In Our Own Way

How Anti-Bias Work Shapes Our Lives

CECELIA ALVARADO ❧ LAVITA BURNLEY ❧ LOUISE DERMAN-SPARKS

ERIC HOFFMAN ❧ LINDA IRENE JIMÉNEZ ❧ JUNE LABYZON

PATRICIA RAMSEY ❧ ANNETTE UNTEN ❧ BETH WALLACE ❧ BARBARA YASUI

Redleaf Press

Published by: Redleaf Press
a division of Resources for Child Caring, Inc.
450 North Syndicate, Suite 5
St. Paul, MN 55104-4125

Distributed by: Gryphon House
Mailing address:
P.O. Box 207
Beltsville, MD 20704-0207

Library of Congress Cataloging-in-Publication Data

In our own way : how anti-bias work shapes our lives / Cecelia
   Alvarado … [et al.].
       p.   cm.
    ISBN 1-884834-50-7
    1. Early childhood education—United States Curricula.
    2. Prejudices—Study and teaching (Early childhood)—United
    States.
    I. Alvarado, Cecelia.
    LB1139.4.I56   1999
    303.3'85'07—dc21   99-27080
                                               CIP

CECELIA ALVARADO
To Yolanda Medina-Garcia and Holly Haws, two of the most inspiring, sensitive, and competent early childhood anti-bias educators I have ever known.

LAVITA BURNLEY
To my children, Brianna and Brian, for the everlasting laughter and joy you share with me, and for my mother, Rebecca, who instilled the courage in me to do my very best.

LOUISE DERMAN-SPARKS
*To Helen Robb, South African activist and anti-bias educator.
Gentle, loving warrior, you live on in our hearts and in our actions.*

ERIC HOFFMAN
*For my colleagues at the Cabrillo College Children's Center and
Early Childhood Education Department.*

LINDA IRENE JIMÉNEZ
To my daughter Amanda-Faye, who inspired my journey; my late grandmothers Trinidad Jiménez and Clara P. Samudio for our culture and warm memories; my immediate family—my parents, sisters, brothers-in-law, nephews, and niece—for their love, support, and strong sense of family; and a special thank you to my great uncle Tío Porfírio Jiménez.

JUNE LABYZON
*To the ones who got me started and won't ever let me stop—the late Ed Miller, Theanette, Dianna, Maggie, Margery and Louise. To "Lloyd" for challenging support.
To the law of Nam Myoho Renge Kyo, the one path to peace.*

PATRICIA RAMSEY
*To Fred, Daniel, and Tuto, for the joys and challenges of being a family
that tries to make a difference.*

ANNETTE UNTEN
*Pu Mehana Kealoha to Tutu Kalama and all the kupunas who have paved the way;
Ernie, Kimo, and Keoni, my life staff; May, Kuulei, Jane, and Paula,
my soul mates on life's journey; and my Circle of Girlfriends, who remind me
that the journey is always worthwhile.*

BETH WALLACE
To the families and teachers at Worcester Child Care Center and Ben & Jerry's Children's Center; and especially to Amethyst Peaslee, Amy Brandt, Andrea Viets, Ann Miller, and Susan Arnowitt-Reid, who talked it all through with me over and over again.

BARBARA YASUI
To Mari and Danny, my reasons for doing this work.

Acknowledgements

This book would never have been born without the brilliant midwifery of Jane Schall, its original editor. Jane is a professional in the truest sense, a person who uses her skill to help others find their voices and grow. Each of the seven teachers whose stories are included was guided by her extraordinary skill, sensitivity, integrity, caring, and patience. She gained the trust of each author, and all of them said that working with Jane throughout the process of writing the book was one of the highlights. Cecelia, Patty, and Louise also give Jane our deepest thanks and respect for bringing to all of us some of the voices of the many practitioners who construct new knowledge about anti-bias work with children everyday and are often never heard outside of their own most immediate circles.

Many thank yous are also necessary to Shelagh Mullings, who transcribed the original interviews that became this book. As Shelagh painstakingly transformed oral history into the first printed drafts, she was also our first reader. When she told us that she cried, cheered, and laughed as she listened to the seven narratives, we knew that many people, regardless of the work they do, would be able to connect with the human journeys of the authors.

Special appreciation goes to the A. L. Mailman Family Foundation, which provided the funds to support the work of creating this book. The foundation's strong commitment and support has been instrumental to the fruition not only of this project, but to a great deal of anti-bias work.

Finally, we thank the families and friends of the seven teachers, who lived with the ups and downs of writing and who often have been the inspiration that kept the seven of them on the anti-bias road.

Table of Contents

Introduction

At the heart of this book are the stories of seven teachers who have examined, challenged, and changed their own lives and their teaching practices to incorporate an anti-bias perspective into their work with children and families. They tell of remarkable yet ordinary lives of pain and triumph, conflict and collaboration, confusion and confidence. The teachers involved are diverse in age, gender, race, culture, class, and sexual orientation, and they work in settings across the country, from rural villages to inner cities. The common thread that ties these stories together is the commitment to understanding issues of bias in contemporary United States society and to apply this understanding to work with children and families.

The stories in this book are fascinating, and you will probably find that you can't put them down. Regardless of experience in the field or current position, early childhood practitioners will find the book a valuable source of information, ideas, and ultimately, support for their own growth in anti-bias work with children. Students preparing for careers in early childhood education can use the stories in this book to envision their future work as teachers. Teacher educators will find in these stories useful examples of professional and personal development to encourage and challenge students. Directors and other administrators will see more clearly how they can influence teachers' efforts to do anti-bias work, as well as how they can create administrative policy and practice that support an anti-bias approach. Parents with children in child care may want to read this book to appreciate the complexities and challenges that child care professionals live with every day. And people who are well along in their careers will gain new perspectives on past events and current challenges as they see the people in these stories confronting similar situations.

In Our Own Way builds on the ideas in *Anti-Bias Curriculum: Tools for Empowering Young Children* by Louise Derman-Sparks and the Anti-Bias Task Force. Published in 1989, this book sparked the current interest in and widespread discussions about anti-bias education. It gave many practitioners both a term and a conceptual framework for shaping the work they were trying to do in the classroom. By illustrating the harmful impact that prejudice and discrimination have on the development of young children, the book introduced thousands of early childhood professionals to a reality they were not aware of or were ignoring. The book reviewed the research showing that children notice diversity and begin to absorb societal bias very early and that early childhood settings are not immune to inequitable and unjust power relationships based on race, culture, gender, physical ability, sexual orientation, and class. Finally, four goals of anti-bias education were identified, all of which apply to adult development as well as to the work that adults do with young children.

The Four Goals of Anti-Bias Education

1. Nurture the construction of a knowledgeable, confident identity as an individual and as a member of multiple identity groups (for example, groups based on gender, race, ethnicity, or class).
2. Promote comfortable, empathetic interaction with people from diverse backgrounds.
3. Foster each child's ability to recognize bias and injustice.
4. Cultivate each child's ability to stand up, individually and with others, against bias or injustice.

The idea for *In Our Own Way* first emerged several years ago in conversations between Louise and Patty about how the anti-bias approach was changing not only teachers' practices with children and families, but also their personal lives and identities. We wanted to create a space for teachers to describe their experiences and transformations in their own voices. As two white women, however, Louise and Patty knew they would bring too narrow a lens to the tasks of choosing contributors and reflecting and interpreting the broad themes that surfaced in their stories. Therefore, they asked Cecelia Alvarado to join them. The final chapter, "Reflecting on the Work of Anti-Bias Educators," integrates our three perspectives about the lessons to be drawn from the contributors' experiences.

Work on the project really began in 1995, when Louise received a grant from the A. L. Mailman Family Foundation. Jane Schall was hired to interview the seven teachers, construct rough drafts of the chapters, and work with the teachers to refine them. Jane spent hours interviewing the authors over the phone. The questions were designed to offer the contributors an opportunity for guided reflection on their anti-bias work, a chance to examine and integrate all of the different influences on their lives and the ways they had responded to the challenge of integrating anti-bias work into their lives. As the interviewing process began, the book took on a life of its own. Jane recalls, "At that point, we had to let go of any preconceived notions and goals and just have faith in the process of people talking to one another, listening to the feelings behind the words, searching for truth and accepting the challenge of self-revelation."

After these taped interviews had been transcribed, Jane created the initial drafts of each chapter and embarked on the lengthy process of revisions. She worked closely with each author, using whatever method they chose to revise their contributions. Some received their chapters on disk and revised on their own. Some made changes and comments on the manuscripts Jane sent them. All of them struggled with similar questions: How much should be said? Who could be hurt? What truths must I stand for? Writing each chapter involved the same soul-searching and risk taking that the authors each demonstrate in their commitment to anti-bias work.

We encourage you to fully immerse yourself in these stories, to try to take on the sense of life location described by each author. Be aware of the context of each author's life and your own internal responses to their stories and ponder why you see the events as you do. Think about experiences you have had that are similar to or different from the ones described here. Imagine how you might respond if confronted by situations similar to these. The discussion questions at the end of each chapter are there for you to use personally or with colleagues or students.

The diversity recorded in these stories reflects the complexity of providing early childhood education that supports all children and families. Not even the whole book, and certainly no one chapter, can tell the whole story of what it means to recognize and begin to address the terrible harm done to children by individual and societal prejudice, bias, and inequity. This book is only a beginning. Many stories remain to be told.

—Cecelia, Louise, and Patty

Annette Unten

Weaving the Pieces Together

*L*ife is a woven tapestry. All the people and the events that enter my life become a part of the threads in my tapestry. Bright colors are woven with pastels. Nubby threads are intertwined with silk and ribbons. All of them add to the richness of this piece. The tapestry will not be complete until I die. What a beautiful tribute to my passage here on earth.

I was born and raised in Hawaii. My mom was of Japanese descent and my dad was Portuguese, Hawaiian, and English. I always say that I was brought up with the strictness of the Japanese culture and the gentleness of the Hawaiian culture—a unique mixture.

I grew up on a sugar plantation in the little town of Waialua on the island of Oahu. It was a really neat place with people from a lot of cultures and a lot of different races. Plantation work didn't pay much, so my dad didn't make a lot of money. My mom worked as a practical nurse and didn't make very much either.

My mom had been married before, outside her race, to a Chinese man. They had two children, my brothers, who she raised alone for two years before she met my dad. Then she married my daddy and had two girls. Perhaps it was the divorce that made her feel so strongly that a woman could be as successful as a man and that a woman could make it on her own. She gave us the message that you shouldn't have to depend on your husband, especially financially, because you can do anything. That message became a part of me and even though I wasn't a super student, I knew I'd go to college. I just knew. Because my mom said I would.

Growing up, I went to a Catholic school where everything was taught from the white culture's perspective. I remember wanting to be white so much, wanting to be blonde and putting a light-colored mop on my head to play white girl. Being white was held up to me as being so special. When it was time to go on to high school, my mom wanted me to continue with a Catholic education, but we couldn't afford it. So I went to the Kamehameha School, where students have to be of Hawaiian ancestry. This school was left by the long line of the Kamehamehas, the last royal family of Hawaii, for the children of Hawaii. At that time, it didn't do much with the Hawaiian culture. All the books and everything else were geared for white students.

When I finished high school, I knew that if I didn't leave Hawaii I would never finish college. A lot of my girlfriends went to the University of Hawaii where the beach is just so lovely that your car automatically drives you there! They all had nice tans—but no degrees. It was still very, very hard to leave. Everything I was used to was there. But I did it. I went to California.

My mom really wanted me to be a nurse. She thought that would mean that I would always have a job. But all I could think was "Ooh, I hate sick people!" And I think the Lord said, "If we make her a nurse, she'll hurt people more than she will help them!" Thank goodness I didn't go to nursing school and

Growing up, I went to a Catholic school where everything was taught from the white culture's perspective. I remember wanting to be white so much, wanting to be blonde and putting a light-colored mop on my head to play white girl.

went into teaching instead. And I have just loved it! That's one thing I'm very clear about. I've taught all ages, from toddlers through college, and I've loved every bit of it.

In California everything was new. Right away, I noticed that my way of dressing was different. It was amazing to me that in California everyone dressed as if there was a change of seasons. All of my clothes were for one season—very loose fitting and casual. That made me stand out.

At first I went to a community college where the teacher in my chemistry class told us that if we had any problems we could come talk to him. So I did. He asked me where I was from, and when I told him Hawaii, he said, "You know, they don't have good schools there. There's no way you're going to pass this class." He was right. I didn't pass. More important, I think that was my first real hit of discrimination. I was being judged by where I grew up.

About that same time, I wanted to join a sorority. There were two on campus. One was the sorority with all the cheerleaders, and that's the one I wanted to be in. The girls there told me, "We think you want the other one, don't you?" At first I didn't get what they meant. At first it didn't hurt. I was again being judged on my appearance, which wasn't their version of a cheerleader.

After I got my associate of arts degree from El Camino College, I went to Cal State Long Beach and received my bachelor's degree. In my fifth year, I earned my elementary teaching credential and, along with that, a specialist credential in early childhood. I went into teaching in 1970 and taught for seven years in the Long Beach School District. Then I had my son, Kimo, and decided to stay home. While Kimo was in preschool, the director asked me to help out. One of the teachers had several children with behavior problems and she thought another person in the room would be great. So I worked part-time. Then she asked me if I'd do a "Mommy and Me" program for the school. I said yes, I would love to. From there, the local junior college asked me to teach in their parent-toddler program. I loved the little ones. There was so much excitement and they were such fun.

I found great joy in this work, but I had also loved college teaching and working with the adults, so I decided to go back and get my master's degree. I started slowly. I had been hearing about Pacific Oaks from different people and decided to visit their campus. When I did, all I could think was: "Oh, boy. This is it. This is where I want to be."

*I*didn't really think a lot about my culture and didn't realize how much I had tried to fit into the white culture until I went to Pacific Oaks. That's when it hit me right between the eyes. In one of my first classes there, taught by Betty Jones, she asked if anyone spoke a language other than English. She knew I was from Hawaii, and when I didn't say anything, she looked at me and said, "Annette, don't you speak Pidgin English?"

I remember looking back at her and thinking, "To hell with that. I'm not going to admit this." Everyone I had ever talked with on the mainland thought that Pidgin English was such an awful language. The subjects don't match the verbs— it was just not considered correct. Then Betty said, "You know Pidgin's a beautiful language, especially if you think of how it came about. It has a little bit of Portuguese, a little bit of Hawaiian, a little bit of Japanese; little bits of this and that so that all people could communicate with each other. It's really great." I could only think, "Oh, my goodness. Nobody's ever said that to me." It felt wonderful.

The Social and Political Contexts class hit me real hard on how racism is a part of society. It answered so many questions that I hadn't been sure about. Puzzle pieces that I thought were missing in my life were in fact there and now began to fit. For instance, there were many things about my Japanese culture that I understood because my mom was the strong personality in our family and brought the Japanese culture into our daily lives. But we didn't do very much with the Hawaiian culture. I think when the government was taken away from the Hawaiian people, the message the people got was that they were not capable of governing themselves. There was also this image on the mainland of Hawaiians spending all their time dancing, singing, and lazing on the beach. I didn't want that image; I didn't want to be part of it. So I used what I could of my own background. If people wanted me to be smart and to the point, then I became Japanese. Since I felt my Hawaiian was not valued, I became "less Hawaiian."

The Social and Political Contexts class hit me real hard on how racism is a part of society. It answered so many questions that I hadn't been sure about. Puzzle pieces that I thought were missing in my life were in fact there and now began to fit.

When I went to Pacific Oaks, I began to see the beauty and gentleness of the Hawaiian culture. I began to see that there's so much to it. And I also began to see that so many incidents in my past—the sorority that wouldn't let me in and the professor who said I'd never learn because I was Hawaiian—played a big part in how I saw myself.

At Pacific Oaks I started asking myself why I was surprised when people pointed me out as being Hawaiian or assumed that I was Asian. I realized that I had been seeing myself as white, as fitting in with everybody else. I began to understand that people just see what they see. And, as I began to be comfortable with who I was, I found myself embracing my Hawaiian side. That brought me back to my hula, to joining a Hawaiian club in California, and wanting our kids to be part of it. At the same time, I was learning that, as a person of color, I needed to be real strong and sure about who I was. If I could do that—if I could be centered—everything else would fall together. But if I couldn't, that's when all the questions and hurts would come up.

🍃

At the same time, I was learning that, as a person of color, I needed to be real strong and sure about who I was. If I could do that— if I could be centered— everything else would fall together. But if I couldn't, that's when all the questions and hurts would come up.

From that point, I moved to a very angry stage where I started fighting every battle. I think it's an important stage to go through. If you try to hide behind the niceties, nothing's ever going to happen and you never get anywhere. So this was a time when I fought. I fought almost everybody. We'd go out to dinner and somebody would make a comment about a black waitress being slow. That was a fight right there. Any stereotype—the Japanese being too strict or too structured, Chicanos being lazy or dirty or field hands—and I'd find myself getting furious. I know I turned a lot of people off. It's just that when I realized that I was a woman of color, it really hit me hard.

Finally, from all that anger came a woman of substance and a woman of strength. I realized that when I spoke in anger, my anger was all the other person heard. And my message was totally lost. I learned that when I tried to move people into action or move diversity forward with my anger, my efforts were useless.

I graduated from Pacific Oaks with a dual specialization— bicultural education and college teaching. I figured that if I worked in a college, I could reach more people who would be teaching children. So that's where I started. I worked adjunct at several colleges and finally got a full-time job at Orange Coast College in California. My credentials were in place. I was cho-

sen because I was the best for the position. But part of me has always wondered how much my being a person of color played a part in the final selection.

I loved the students. And I loved college teaching. When I taught my class on diversity, I could feel myself grow. And I began to really understand that if you want to teach diversity, you really, really have to work on yourself. You have to look heavily into yourself.

I was teaching college and doing diversity workshops. I was getting so much support from our anti-bias support group. I was in my element. Then recession hit Orange County and my husband, Ernie, lost his job.

My job was secure. I loved it and felt that it was one I could retire in. When a job opportunity for Ernie came up in Texas, I said to him, "Go check it out," because I knew Ernie wouldn't be foolish enough to take a job in Texas. Well, he did. I said to him, "Leave me and the boys here for one year and see if you really like it there." And this time Ernie said no, he wanted us together as a family. And so off we went to Texas.

It was a difficult time in my life. I didn't want to leave college teaching and especially my diversity work. I was part of the CAEYC Anti-Bias Leadership Internship Program, and that was really important to me. I talked with Louise about continuing my internship, and she said that I could. This made me feel a little better.

But I was angry that all my hard work toward getting the college position was for naught. After working so hard to get my full-time faculty position in California, breaking into the Texas system would be extremely difficult. I did not want to do years of adjunct work to prove myself again. And I needed support to do the diversity work. Who would be my support in Texas? I felt lost and didn't have focus.

When I arrived in Texas I needed to find a job to help with the family finances, so I went back to elementary education. I started my job search in the middle of October, and a position opened up in the same district my children were in. What do you think? A Pre-K position, the best, fell in my lap.

Being back in the classroom after teaching in college has been a very humbling and enlightening experience for me. It forced me to walk the talk after those years in a college classroom teaching people what they should do. I know that if I ever go back to teaching college, I will be better at it because of this experience. Being back in the classroom, I've also realized that teaching is really about a teacher's growth and reflections. And this constant growth, looking at things in different ways, is what keeps teachers excited and in love with teaching. I know it does for me. If you're aware of it, diversity hits you every day. If you stay centered, you are open to all the new ideas that come into your classroom from the children you work with. If you stay centered, you are able to ask yourself important questions.

Some of my questions now come from the awareness that culture is a big part of the classroom. The children come to us and they have to get acclimated to a new culture—the school—that is many times different from home. I find myself asking: Do we allow enough time for their growth? How can we help?

Most recently I have been asking, Have we really looked at still another important factor—the teacher's culture? How does it affect the classroom? How does it affect anti-bias teaching? This is so important. Whether we like it or not, each of us is influenced not just by our ethnic, racial, or religious background, but by all the components of how we grew up. And that can certainly influence our expectations of the children we work with and the kind of guidance we offer.

Most recently I have been asking, Have we really looked at still another important factor—the teacher's culture? How does it affect the classroom? How does it affect anti-bias teaching? This is so important.

I know of a teacher who got so angry at a child because of the way he was walking—the same kind of a swagger we did in Hawaii growing up. She thought it showed disrespect. When she pulled the child aside, I could hear the teacher's parents saying to her, "When you walk away from me, never walk like that!" What messages is she passing on?

That teacher isn't alone. I grew up where showing respect for an adult is really important. We never called an adult by his or her first name, so it was very hard for me when I worked at a school where students did that. When I talked with a child, I expected the kind of respect I associated with "Mr.," "Mrs.," or whatever. That was my culture. And now I understand that how I expect a child to respond may not be the same as what is expected in that child's home culture. I've found that I have to be real careful to reflect on what I'm doing and not to make assumptions.

What happens when a child comes into my room with a totally different culture than mine? How do we both grow? I don't have all the answers, but I know that we can do the best possible job only if we have looked inside ourselves.

But even that isn't enough. There are always questions we need to ask ourselves to understand each situation better: What was my role as a student? What were my parents' expectations of me? What did my parents expect their role was going to be in my schooling?

Then we need to look closely at how our answers influence the way we manage our classrooms, interact with the children, and determine the expectations we place on their parents. Taking this another step, we need to ask, What happens when a child comes into my room with a totally different culture than mine? How do we both grow? I don't have all the answers, but I know that we can do the best possible job only if we have looked inside ourselves.

This self-reflection is especially important when you have children of color in your room. Starting with all the richness of their cultures is basic. Helping them grow and teaching them the best ways to interact in the main culture is essential. If we don't, we limit their access to many opportunities and, often, their chances for success. That's been true in our bilingual program where the children are kept in separate classes all the way through fourth grade. In my opinion, this isn't fair because in a few years they will no longer be separated and we will not have done our job to help them succeed. So here are some questions I'm asking: What are our goals for the children? Is the program working? What do parents want? Who is benefiting from this program the way it works right now?

As teachers, we bring with us years of experience, greatly influenced by the culture we grew up in. We must reflect on who we are and how much our expectations are steeped in our own culture.

I think that the only way an individual can become aware of his or her culture is through a process of reflection, action, and self-growth. About three years ago I started looking into and centering myself. I have also just started a women's support group called the Circle of Girlfriends. It is our journey toward empowerment. I feel strongly that women are the only ones who can empower each other. Men can't do this for women. The women in my group are open to growth and don't need constant pats on the back from others. Much of our power comes from within, and through the group we are able to share it.

When I arrived in Texas, I didn't know anyone who was doing anti-bias work. I was really alone, and I remember thinking: I can't do this. I just can't. (At the time, I didn't realize that because I was already committed inside, I just didn't really have a choice.) I began to read books that dealt with

questions on topics such as women's issues and different ways to teach children. I also started a journal. Journals are such a reward, like a gift, because they help you see the growth, even a few months down the line. Sometimes you're worried you haven't grown at all and you're almost afraid to look back, but then you read your journal and the growth is so obvious. A journal reaffirms all of your anti-bias work, the tough things and the great things. It doesn't have to be shared. No one else ever has to read it. You don't have to write in it everyday. And when you do, it can be just one thought or observation.

To begin a journal entry, I might ask myself: What is a question that came up for me today? Why was it so difficult with this child? What are my feelings about this situation? What part does my culture play? How does that make the child feel? If I were the child, what would I be learning from this? I also start asking others these same questions, often in the teachers' lounge. It helps me to hear the questions out loud and listen to people's responses and their discussions. A person interested in asking questions will be open to many things. I found people to be a part of the Circle of Girlfriends in this way. It's been terrific. We're starting simply. We ask ourselves a question a week. The first question is, Who do I say I am? This doesn't mean who you are from anyone else's point of view. Only your own. From there we will keep going, keep looking inside ourselves, and keep growing.

I've always believed that people are capable of growing. But I've learned, through a lot of mistakes, that people have to grow at their own rates and in their own ways and that no one is going to grow like me. There was a time when I wanted to force growth, a time when I felt there had to be a formula. Now I am aware that we all grow differently, and I am able to appreciate and listen to people who are at various stages of growth. Basically, I believe that everybody is on a growth path.

After our move to Texas, I was scared that my personal growth was diminishing. Support from the Circle of Girlfriends has given me access to growth and renewed my faith in my own abilities. In the Circle of Girlfriends we challenge each other to grow, asking each other questions to help us see new perspectives in nonthreatening ways. I then bring that growth to my teaching. Years ago, rather than question, I would make assumptions. For instance, if there was a problem in class, it was the child's problem. I even blamed the parents, where they lived, or the circumstances. The biggest growth for me has been gaining the confidence to question situations. Rather than making assumptions, I now ask, Where is my bias in this? What do I need to do to make things happen so this child can grow?

Blame, I've found, doesn't help anything change, and neither do assumptions—especially mine. Working in my support group has opened me up to asking questions of myself that I didn't ask before. After all, I was so smart. I loved the children I taught and wanted to be a good teacher. These were good reasons for continuing with my work. But when you work with a support group and with yourself, they're not enough.

When I find myself struggling, I know that I have to pull back and say to myself, "There's a question here and I'm not listening to it." Then, somewhere along the line, I begin to share my concerns. I begin to ask more questions. And the journey toward growth continues.

To people just starting out in diversity work, I'd like to say this: Make the physical changes first. Change the books in your room, the toys, and the pictures. These are changes you can make right away. That's important. The work you do later will not always be so visible, but there will be a thrill to doing it. In fact, there will be many feelings (fear, excitement, frustration, disappointment, anticipation) because the work is so complex.

I've found that one way to bring anti-bias teaching into my pre-K classroom is to look for openings rather than trying to create them. For instance, one of my students, Tracy, came in on a Monday and quietly said to me, "Mrs. Unten, I was in a parade this weekend."

"You were?" I said.

"Yeah. It was kind of for black people. It was a neat parade. It was for Martin Luther King."

"That's wonderful," I said. "Dr. Martin Luther King was a really great man. It's wonderful that you were in a parade for him." Then I added, "You know there were a lot of black people there because Martin Luther King was black and he did so many wonderful things for black people. He did many wonderful things for white people too. That's something that we should talk about more."

Upon reflection, I realized this little boy thought that this wasn't an event he could share with everyone—maybe he thought he could just talk to black people about it. So I used our conversation as an opening to read everyone a story about Martin Luther King and his life. It helped Tracy feel comfortable sharing something that had been important to him. That's how it happens.

Here's another example of how I was able to bring anti-bias teaching into my class by using the openings that the children create. I overheard two black girls talking in the housekeeping area. One said to the other, "White girls talk like this…" and she mimicked a voice that was slow and kind of sweet.

I listened and then asked, "Simone, how do black girls speak?"

"Black girls, they…" and she made her speech have much more rhythm.

"That's interesting," I said. "It seems like we speak differently. How do I speak?" So she started imitating me perfectly. (I just wanted to crack up.) We talked about that and then I asked her how the other adult in our room, Mrs. Houchen,

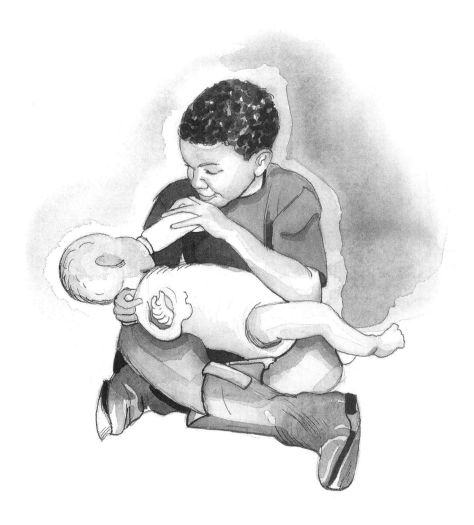

speaks. Simone had it down to a science. Then we moved on to different people in our class, particularly a girl named Michelle, who was white. I asked her, "Is that how Michelle speaks?"

"No," she said, "She don't speak like that."

"But I thought that was how white girls speak."

"Well, Michelle don't speak like that. Is she white?" Simone is bright and, as we continued to talk, she began to realize that skin color isn't what makes people speak differently from one another.

That is one of the reasons working in early childhood is so wonderful. You have time to spend together and you can use the openings that the children provide to make diversity discussions a natural part of conversations. In this case, Simone and I sat down to talk and everybody in the housekeeping area kind of listened. Our conversation became a lesson for many of those children. I think that a lot of things happen in my classroom like that.

And I believe, when people feel accepted for who they are and are accepting of themselves, they're more willing to accept others who are different.

Another way to encourage children's growth is to introduce a concept and then let them take it wherever they can. For instance, we talk about skin color because I really believe it's so important. Growing up, nobody ever said anything to me like: "Annette, the color of your skin is just beautiful" or "That brown color is just so pretty." And that contributed to why I always wanted to be white. So I like to tell all the children that their skin color is pretty and just right for them. We draw pictures of ourselves and match skin colors. We talk about different colors of skin. From there, lots of incidents just happen. For instance, we couldn't find the dolls when school started this year. We finally found a few to put out, mostly little tiny dolls of color. But of the big dolls, I only had one and she was white. Early in the year, one of my students, Antoinette, who is black, looked up and said, "I was wonderin', Mrs. Unten, why you don't have my dolly out there. You have other people's dollies, but you don't have mine." She had been looking for the black doll. That's the one she wanted, not the white doll. We looked together and she spotted it way back in the closet. So we got it out and found some clothes for her. It was too important not to.

My job is easier because I have such diversity in my class. We have time to sit together, share, and talk about differences, and most of the time, everyone is represented in some way. In addition, early childhood lends itself to talking about diversity. Children's developmental ages are ripe for growth at this time. They're very, very open. And, over the course of a year, I can see much growth in the ways they treat each other and how they interact. All you have to do in a classroom like mine is offer opportunities through the books that we read and what we show about being accepting of who we are and where we are. For instance, a lot of my children don't have daddies. So every time we read a book or we talk about families, we make sure we show mommies without daddies. That helps children feel accepted. And I believe, when people feel accepted for who they are and are accepting of themselves, they're more willing to accept others who are different.

As I said, I'm hit with diversity every day in countless little incidents that just come up. Diversity is just a part of what we do. It's so natural that it's hard for me to separate anti-bias work from everything else or to think of what I do that's different.

*E*very year I ride home on the bus with the children. Seeing where they live helps me to focus, to remember what they have to go home to. The families in our program are really poor. Many have no screens on their windows. Many doors are kicked in. I know when the children come to school in the mornings, many haven't had a warm bed to sleep in. The bus ride pulls me together and reminds me about what I have to do. It reminds me that sometimes the openings I observe are really for my own awareness and growth. For example, the other day my aide and I were observing the housekeeping area. The children hadn't been using the table and everything was on the floor—including the food they had set out. My aide wondered why and that's when it occurred to me that probably the children didn't have a table at home. As every early childhood person knows, what children see at home is often what they model in the housekeeping corner.

About four days later one of the girls, Tracharia, came in with newspapers in her hand. She said "Here, Mrs. Unten, I have some newspapers to bring to school." I said, "That's great. What shall we do with this newspaper? Where shall we put it? Shall we put it with the books in the book corner?" "No," she said. "It goes in housekeeping." I said, "Okay, that sounds fine to me. Let's put it in housekeeping." I thought Tracharia meant they would read it in housekeeping. No. When it was time for centers, Tracharia spread the newspaper on the floor like a tablecloth so that it would keep the play food clean. These kinds of things happen daily.

Diversity makes you aware that things are not always as you assume. It challenges your paradigm and makes you grow. Over the years, I have had many opportunities. And at the end of each year I sit back and ask myself, What have I learned? What have I gained? How have I grown? And I always come out the winner.

*T*o do the work you need support. You cannot do this kind of job by yourself. To keep myself going, I always have to find a soul mate. That isn't always easy. I know it may take me a little while. If I am open, then I know it's going to happen. I think my growth has tripled recently because I have found someone to grow with. Her name is Paula.

You get to really love your soul mate. For me, Paula has been the most wonderful person to grow with. We have grown spiritually, and I believe this has opened up my mental capacity to learn new things and to be open to new people. I feel more strongly than ever that women empower women differently than men do.

Someone said teaching is not a profession; it's a calling. That is really, really true. The more you find support, the more you can keep growing. The more you hear the calling, the more exciting it is to teach. If you're reaching that tired stage a lot of times it's because things are stagnant in your life. So you have to be real selfish, go after support, and look for that growth. It does come back. It comes back and gets really exciting again. You just can't do it by yourself.

I also rely on the children's parents for support. For a few years now, I have called every parent the first week of school. I'll make five or so calls every day. I just call to talk. If I get a machine, I say, "This is Mrs. Unten. I'm DJ's teacher and I just wanted to let you know that he's doing a wonderful job in class." When they hear that, they pick up the phone. Many of them tell me that teachers never call unless there's something bad to talk about. That's why having a teacher call is scary for them.

I begin each call by thanking them for doing a good job of raising their children. I honestly believe that they're doing the very best they can. It's a belief that comes from my heart. With a beginning like that, we can go on together because we're already supporting each other; we already have a past. That's part of building trust. And once you have it, there isn't anything a parent wouldn't do for you. I treasure this good rapport with my parents. It's an invaluable source of support for me.

I find that the more work I've done on myself, the more the world opens up. I use to keep things in categories. My teaching was separate from my home life. My home life was separate from my growth in meditation. And my support group was separate from everything else. I now know the times that I enjoy most are the moments when I reflect on my teaching day and see how the anti-bias curriculum has become an intricate part of everything I do. These moments affirm for me that this is how I interact with the world. My teaching, home life, support group, and creativity are now all connected. Through anti-bias work, my life has become whole.

I've come to realize that my mom, who was so strict with me growing up, had the most difficult job of raising us. Now I see that Daddy's job was easier. Come love me, kiss me, squeeze me. We all ran to him. But Mama was the meanie, pulling us in, making us toe the line.

There's so much that you see when you're older. There so much you can forgive yourself for, and so forgive others too. You can look at something with love that you never could see before. It's good to grow old and reflect on that. It's good to be at this stage. I don't ever want to be young again. I'm in such a good place now, a place where I can be more open with my two sons. I think that Keoni and Kimo are lucky to have me at this stage of my growth.

My husband, Ernie, has been very supportive all along. He's been wonderful because he really does embrace and love the Hawaiian culture, though he is not of Hawaiian descent. He's Okinawan. When we joined the Hawaiian Club in California, much to my surprise, he was even one of the best male dancers. He has always been so together as a person. He's never felt threatened by my growth. When I decided to go back to school at age forty, he said, "Honey, if it's important to you, go and I will do whatever I need to do to support you." So Ernie took care of all the birthday parties and all the slumber parties. He cooked and cleaned and became a great sounding board for my growth, even though he may not have agreed with all of my diversity philosophy, especially when I was at the arguing stage. He's heard and absorbed so much living with me that now he's noticing bias in everything.

Diversity has helped me see how great my kids are. Observing and allowing them to grow has been really special. Keoni, my younger son, is going through young adolescence and noticing differences between him and his friends. He's asking questions and testing his voice on issues. That's where he is in the diversity process. I tell Kimo, my eighteen-year-old son, that I'm not all-knowing. It's my turn to let go and listen to what he has to say. And when I do, I can see the blessing that he is.

In thinking about my own journey, I've realized there was no set timetable. My journey evolved. If you stay committed, yours will too. So be wary of timetables. They are subject to so many variables—where you teach, the people around you, the children you have each year. Don't compare yourself to anyone else, because every journey is different. This journey is only yours. And remember, don't be too hard on yourself. Any work that you do on yourself will be greatly reflected in your teaching.

Anti-bias has become an integral part of my woven tapestry of life. For me, this journey is kept alive and challenging as I work on my own personal growth. I realize that I don't need to know all the answers. But I have to have the questions. And then, as I get further along, I can share.

Since the process of writing this book began, the Circle of Girlfriends has continued to blossom and grow. Quietly, passionately, changes are being made in our school and among ourselves. Blessings continue to flow. I am doing workshops on diversity issues in the surrounding school districts and for the PBS station in Austin, Texas.

And so the weaving continues.

Discussion Questions

1. Annette talks about wanting to be white as a young child. What do you see in our society (in stores, media, literature, and so on) that would make children of color feel this way?

2. Annette says that diversity comes up every day in her classroom. Observe a child care center or a preschool class for a full day and keep a list of all the ways diversity comes up among the children.

3. Annette speaks of learning through deep reflection how our own culture affects our expectations and assumptions about children. How do you see your own culturally specific values influencing your perceptions of children, especially those who come from a culture different from yours?

Linda Irene Jiménez
Finding a Voice

My father's parents crossed the Mexico/U.S.A. border in 1920 when my grandmother was pregnant because they wanted a better life for their children. When I was a kid, I often heard the word *wetbacks* used when whites addressed Mexicans or Mexican Americans, but I didn't know that many Mexican people swam across the Rio Grande to get to the United States and the term came from this. As a child I had always assumed that my abuelito and abuelita had lived in Texas all their lives. When I got older and understood what the term really meant, it hurt when people called me that. You see, it seemed unfair that people had risked their lives for a better life in this country and in return were put down for it.

My maternal grandparents, on the other hand, were born in Texas. Though American, they still didn't have the opportunity to attend school. Grandma Clara, my maternal grandmother, more than anything wanted to learn to read and write in English. Before her death in 1973, she was able to sign her name instead of just writing an X. She also learned, with her grandchildren's help, to speak basic English and write simple three-letter words. She was as proud of those accomplishments as she was of seeing some of her grandchildren graduate from high school and attend college.

I consider myself a feminist, and I think my paternal grandmother, buelita Trinidad, would have been one also. She was not the typical female of her time. As a matter of fact, she was ahead of her time. She did things that other Mexican women didn't do. She watched out for herself and believed it was important not to allow a male to mistreat you. And she was a character. When I think of developing my voice, I think of a story about her. Now it's funny, but at the time it was embarrassing.

I have so many memories and stories about my grandmothers and paternal grandfather. I don't think I appreciated them as much as I do now that I have embarked on reclaiming my culture. Now I see my grandparents as role models.

You see, my buelita wore dentures and she was always careless about where she put them, unlike Grandma Clara who placed hers carefully in a glass of water whenever she was not wearing them. One day when buelita couldn't find them, she called the Spanish radio station and asked them to announce that if anyone found her dentures could they please be returned to her! When my sisters, cousins, and my aunt heard the broadcast, we just about died. "Ay, buelita, why did you do that?" Her response was, "Hey, I need my teeth." I don't believe anyone else of that time, especially a female, would have done that!

My abuelita was also a church-going person; she attended mass daily, yet she also cursed and smoked. As a kid I thought that was really neat. I especially liked the way she held her cigarette between her thumb and index finger while she took long drags.

I have so many memories and stories about my grandmothers and paternal grandfather. (I didn't see my maternal grandfather very often.) I don't think I appreciated them as much as I do now that I have embarked on reclaiming my culture. Now I see my grandparents as role models.

Some of the memories are painful. I know I was influenced by dominant culture messages about looksism, and consequently at times wasn't fair to my buelita. She was short, stocky, and dark-skinned. Grandma Clara was taller and slimmer, with lighter skin. Buelita wore her hair in long braids, while Grandma Clara's hair was shorter and more stylish. Buelita always wore an apron; Grandma Clara took much pride in making her clothes and would wear hats and gloves to church on Sundays. Buelita was not a tidy housekeeper, while Grandma was immaculately clean. To this day, the smell of White Shoulders cologne—Grandma Clara's favorite—makes me think of her and visualize her perfectly organized dresser drawers. When it came to gift giving, I was unfair to my buelita. I usually gave the "prettier" gift to Grandma Clara because I thought she was prettier. But now, looking back, I can see that although they were different in many ways, both my grandmothers struggled in society.

Buelita and buelito owned a mom-and-pop store across the street from the Catholic church in our barrio, thus they were well known in our community. Buelito worked for the Santa Fe Railroad, so buelita ran the store while he was at work. Although her English was limited, she would not shy away from trying her best to communicate when accepting deliveries or ordering goods. And the deliverymen just adored her. I admired her for not being ashamed of her accent when she tried to speak English, especially since white people often mocked this. But my buelita felt she was not pretty because her skin was dark. I remember her telling me that I was pretty because I had light skin.

Grandma Clara was orphaned as an infant and raised by relatives. Her recollections of childhood were of growing up poor. Her philosophy was, "It doesn't matter how poor you are, there's no excuse for being dirty." So as a young girl she learned how to sew her clothes from flour sacks. She felt that having the ability to sew, along with the fact that soap was not expensive, made it possible to always look presentable. I also remember her looking at books and magazines every day, and we would hear her say, "If I could read, I think I would read all the time." So even though she couldn't read the instructions, she was forever ordering crochet and quilting books. When they came she would look at the pictures and count the loops to crochet or make her own patterns for quilting and use remnants from the dresses she made.

I really miss my grandmothers. I think of them often, especially in my current living situation. I purchased a home with one of my sisters and it's ironic, we are like the odd couple—Oscar and Felix or buelita and Grandma. I am like buelita Trini and my sister is like Grandma Clara. They are an important part of my story.

I was born in west Texas and our family lived in the barrio. My parents were working class. My father worked for a meatpacking company and my mother worked at a dry cleaners. I liked it when she didn't have to work because we always came home to a warm house full of nice aromas from whatever she was cooking.

Our neighborhood was predominately Mexican and Mexican American. We attended school in the barrio from first to third grade. After that we went to an integrated school—Mexicans and whites. For me the transition occurred during the 1960–1961 school year. Before attending this new school, I had heard stories about kids being made fun of for taking tortillas for lunch, so it was either white bread sandwiches or purchasing food at the cafeteria for me. (Actually, there were also stories about a teacher who would trade his sandwiches for tortillas. That guy must have known what good food was all about!) It was a struggle because we wanted to fit in and not be made fun of because of our differences.

I had learned that we were different at a very young age. I remember a time in the mid-fifties when my parents, my three sisters, and I went to Sears. My sisters and I were thirsty so we

looked for a drinking fountain. We found two—side by side. On one was a sign that read "Whites Only," the other one read "Colored Only." Why wasn't there a drinking fountain for us? Which should we drink from? We knew that we were not "white" because our kind was not allowed admittance at certain parks or restaurants. And we knew "colored" was a reference to blacks. What would happen if we drank from the "Colored Only" one? At that age, we wondered if our skin would turn black or if our lips would get bigger. My sister Becky was like the Mikey of the cereal commercials—she volunteered. As she drank she turned toward us and we watched for a transformation. "Is anything happening to me?" she asked. To our amazement, there was no change! We never questioned what would happen if we drank from the "Whites Only" fountain.

My parents experienced prejudice frequently and really did not want to expose us to it. I remember overhearing conversations between them about the discrimination they and other people around us experienced. For example, my mother's father was a light-skinned Latino who was born in Texas and spoke English well. He had two brothers whose skin was darker than his. He was consistently treated differently than they were in public. Once, the three of them went into a barbershop and the barber refused to cut the two brothers' hair, but because he thought my grandfather was white, he was willing to cut his hair. Whenever my grandfather went to the movie theater alone or with white friends, he was allowed to sit downstairs, but when he went with his brothers or other dark-skinned friends, he was required to sit in the balcony. Simply speaking Spanish in a public place would often result in a person's being asked to leave. Once my grandfather and his brothers went to eat in a restaurant. They were speaking English, and then after they had ordered, they started conversing in Spanish. They were asked to leave. Incidents like these occurred regularly to people in our family or other people we knew—they were just a fact of life.

My parents tried their best to explain things like the "Whites Only" fountain, and also to shelter us from the racism around us. They told us that even though we were Mexican American, we were lumped in with Caucasians and were considered white. It was difficult to understand this because of the blatant prejudice and discrimination that we faced in our daily lives.

The summer prior to my sixth-grade year, a new Catholic school was built in the affluent area of town. At mass, our priest announced that if kids from the barrio were interested in attending, they would provide a bus for transportation. My youngest sister and I decided we wanted to go, along with about fifteen other kids.

Almost immediately I knew I didn't like it and didn't want to continue. I could see and feel the prejudice. I had attended catechism classes weekly from the time I was in first grade and the nuns, for the most part, were good to us. They taught us that Jesus loved all the children in the world—white, black, brown, red, and yellow. At this school, however, the nuns weren't very nice to the kids of color, especially Mother Superior (who was the principal and teacher of my combination sixth- and seventh-grade class). Many of the white kids were from wealthy families, and many from the local air force base were transported in a much nicer bus. Our very old yellow school bus broke down almost daily. We were ridiculed again and again.

During the ten-minute period in which we changed classrooms, the teachers stood outside their door-ways. If they heard anyone speaking Spanish, they would make that person stay after school and write "I will not speak Spanish at school" on the chalkboard one hundred times. The message was clear to me—being Mexican and speaking Spanish was not okay.

At that school there was a Mexican family with five children—three girls and two boys. The girls wore their hair in the long traditional braids with ribbons woven into them. Sometimes they also wore the pretty white Mexican blouses with the ruffle along the neckline and shoulders. Their mother, a tall, large woman who also wore her hair in long braids, walked with great pride as she delivered a platter of warm burritos each day for her children's lunch. I would cringe with embarrassment for them because other kids made fun. But they weren't ashamed at all.

The youngest boy in that family, Armando, was in kindergarten. He was just learning English. Mother Superior would take turns bringing him and another kindergartner, Kevin, to our room to visit. Kevin was the son of an Air Force major, very articulate for his age—and, of course, English was his first language. She would sit each boy in front of the class and ask him questions. When Kevin was there everyone oohed and aahed over his answers. He was just so cute and smart! But Armando, who didn't even understand many of the questions, would respond in his broken English with a Spanish accent and the class would laugh. I remember feeling so much hurt and humiliation for him. I think this was the beginning of a lot of anger brewing inside of me. I can honestly say that at that period of my life I hated the church and the nuns.

So I told my parents that I no longer wanted to attend that school. I remember not being able to tell them exactly what was going on. Culturally, I suppose, I felt I could not question what the church did. My mother felt that I shouldn't be a quitter, and since I was the one who had decided to go there in the first place, she felt strongly that I had to finish the year. It was very difficult and painful. Ironically, up until that time I had entertained the idea of becoming a nun.

The following year I attended a public junior high school in a white neighborhood, which was also integrated. This was my first experience in having a different teacher for every subject. During the ten-minute period in which we changed classrooms, the teachers stood outside their doorways. If they heard anyone speaking Spanish, they would make that person stay after school and write "I will not speak Spanish at school" on the chalkboard one hundred times. The message was clear to me—being Mexican and speaking Spanish was not okay. I wanted so much to fit in, as I'm sure many others did too.

Later that year we moved to California. That was very hard for me. I didn't want to leave my neighborhood and family. But my mother wanted more opportunities for her daughters and felt that a new life in California could give us that. I remember crying for one whole year that I wanted to go back to Texas. It was such a harsh adjustment to make.

In my new school, the enrollment again consisted of whites and Latinos. And there, like in Texas, I was on a roller coaster ride—at times hating being Mexican and wanting to be white, and at other times wanting to be proud of who I was and hating whites for what they had done to me. I had a good friend who was born in Mexico. She and her family raved about their country and heritage. It made me wish that Mexico was my birth country as well.

Throughout high school I was very unhappy and was always complaining of chest pains. In my senior year, my parents insisted that I see a doctor, and she referred me to a therapist. In 1969, seeing a therapist was not the "in" thing to do. I felt that I was viewed as being crazy, but I think that woman saved my life. We worked on several issues, but I always had a nagging feeling that there was something in me trying to emerge. It would also come up in my dreams, but I couldn't pin it down.

I connected with Pacific Oaks College when I began looking for a program for my daughter, Amanda-Faye. She was an infant and I needed to be with other adults, especially other mommies, so I called Pacific Oaks about their infant/toddler program and was invited to visit. It felt uncomfortable. Although there was a handful of women of color, most of the other moms were white and middle class. However, despite my uneasiness, I also felt an attraction. You see, deep down inside, I still wished I was white. I thought it would make me fit in better in that environment.

When I was told that they offered scholarships, I felt like they thought of me as a "welfare case." I didn't realize then that the school was truly trying to diversify the child care student population by offering scholarships to people of color and working-class people. I took pride in working and paying for my expenditures. It was a reflection of my parents' attitude about the work ethic and of the fact that I had bought into the system's negative attitude about people on assistance.

I asked for an application and hesitantly mailed it back two days before the deadline. They called immediately offering the scholarship and we were enrolled when Amanda-Faye was three months old. While the babies interacted in the environment and with the staff, the parents (usually moms) met to discuss parenting issues. I found it fascinating, especially when we talked about issues that I could not relate to, like their problems with the help who lived in their guesthouses. I was a single working-class mom who lived with my parents and shared a room with my daughter. However, for the most part, there were issues common to all of us. And, for a while, there was a support group for single moms once a week in the evenings. Most of the discussions in that group were relevant to me in so many ways.

There were also general parent meetings for the entire Pacific Oaks Children's School. I remember one meeting in particular where the topic was "Racism and Sexism in Children's Literature." During that meeting I became more aware of children's book illustrations and content. I learned that even though an author's intention might not be racist or sexist, the way something was illustrated or written could encourage those attitudes. To my dismay, several books that I enjoyed reading to children fell in this category. Even an alphabet book could be racist—for example, the illustration for the letter "I" showing a stereotype of an American Indian dancing around a fire wearing skimpy clothes, a feathered headband, war paint on his face, and holding a tomahawk.

Amanda-Faye was verbal at a very young age. Once, in the two-year-old yard, I yelled at her for something. She looked up at me and said, "When you yell at me, Mommy, it really hurts my ears. You can do one of two things. You can tell me in a nice voice or not tell me at all. What is your decision?" I was dumbfounded. Here was my child telling me how it felt when I yelled at her and giving me a choice. I knew that what she was saying came from the things that were said to her. It was so empowering—to this little child, and to me!

I used to go in early to pick up Amanda-Faye so I could stay to observe. At the time, I often felt embarrassed because I had an accent and couldn't pronounce some English words properly. One day I decided to stay for story time. Mohammed, one of the teachers, was reading a book and he mispronounced some of the words. When the preschool-age children started giggling, he put the book down gently and said, "I want to tell you that I come from a country called Iran and we speak Farsi there. English is my second language, and many of the words are difficult for me. When I make a mistake and people laugh at me, it hurts my feelings. It's okay if you will help me say them right." He was so gentle in his delivery. From the look on the children's faces, I could see that they understood. From then on, when I would hear Mohammed reading and making a mistake, I would also hear the children say, "Mohammed, that's not the right way. This is how you say it." Then he would thank them for their help. I realized that it didn't matter that I was born in America and

still mispronounced words. I decided to try Mohammed's technique with adults and children and found that it really generated respect and understanding.

What longed to be free in me actually emerged at another meeting at Pacific Oaks Children's School. Louise Derman-Sparks and the Anti-Bias Task Force had been developing the anti-bias curriculum and some of the task force members were incorporating the curriculum into the children's programs. They had informed the parents about it and the predominantly white parent population was up in arms. They were particularly concerned about the issue of race. They felt that making children aware of racial differences would only encourage prejudice. After all, three and four year olds did not notice color, so those parents believed.

As the parents strongly voiced their concerns and objections, I visualized my empowered almost four-year-old

Amanda, who was a testimonial for all that they were opposing. It was Amanda-Faye, at age two and a half, who had said, "You know Mommy, you don't have to be a girl to like pink and a boy to like blue. Girls can like blue and boys can like pink." She also shared this with her grandfather as they frosted a cake for my cousin's baby. It was Amanda-Faye who decided to be a fancy, glittery, rich witch on Halloween. She chose black fabric and insisted that I add rhinestones and glitter to the dress and the veil of her hat. Another girl dressed as Glinda, the witch from the Wizard of Oz. She chose a pink gown that was quite striking with her blonde hair. I remember her mother asking the girls, "Can I take a picture of the good witch and the bad witch?" And Amanda-Faye immediately put out her little hand in a stopping motion and declared, "Excuse me, I'm not a bad witch. I'm a good witch. You know it's okay for good witches to wear black." Later on she informed me, "You know, Mommy, judges are good and they wear black. One of these days when I become a judge, I am going to change things and make them fair. Devil's food cake will be white and angel food cake will be chocolate. The good guys will wear black and the bad guys will wear white. The good Shira dolls will have black hair and the bad Shira dolls will have blonde hair."

And it was Amanda who came home at Thanksgiving time and stated, "Christopher Columbus was not a fair guy." After a bit of probing, she added, "He made a big mistake. Queen Isabella sent him to the Indies, but he landed in America and called the people Indians. They're not Indians, they're Native Americans. And those pilgrim people are not fair. The Indians taught them how to plant food and how to build houses, and then they were mean to them and they took everything away."

At the parent meeting, all of these examples flashed in my mind and I started to cry. Everything that Louise was trying to explain to the rest of the parents made so much sense to me. Here was my daughter, a girl of color, who was so empowered. She was aware of "fair" and "unfair," of likenesses and differences. She had the skill to think critically, and she had a voice to express her thoughts and take action. For me, all of this spelled empowerment and validation. And that night I felt I was empowered and validated by Louise Derman-Sparks—a white Jewish woman. It was the beginning of my emergence, the beginning of my reclaiming my culture, developing my voice, and becoming empowered. Because to me, the anti-bias curriculum is based on something that is so basic and important—the issue of respect.

Later, because I was teaching young children myself, Louise invited me to join an anti-bias curriculum support group she was starting. That was another beginning for me, one of commitment in the areas of diversity and anti-racist work. Again, I was frightened and intimidated by some of the participants. Later, I would find out they felt the same way. When Rosa, another Chicana in the group, would question Louise, I would think to myself, "What a troublemaker." Now, as I look back, I realize I wouldn't have labeled her a troublemaker if she had been white. At the time, I just prayed that she wouldn't question anything I said. But little by little I started to realize that I was threatened by her because she was my color. I think I was envious that I did not possess her "voice." Later, on a flight to a conference where we would co-present, we shared our life stories and found we had similar childhood experiences. I had been so naive. Her ability to speak up and question had taken years to develop. And now I can chuckle about my feelings. Even though Rosa has moved out of state, we talk to each other at least once a year. Our conversations challenge my thinking and empower me.

Over time in this process, I've learned to be honest about who and what I am. Consequently, I have been able to delve deeper, open up, grow, and make allies. Shutting people out just keeps you from being able to peel back through all the layers of bias and misunderstanding.

Our anti-bias curriculum support group met every two weeks for ten months. We covered each chapter of the *Anti-Bias Curriculum* book, engaged in self-awareness activities, discussed personal issues that were stumbling blocks, and presented activities in our classrooms. We also talked about people with disabilities, which was one area that was difficult for me. It brought back memories of first grade. I was in elementary school in the fifties, when many children and adults had polio and I always feared that I would get it. There was a girl in my class who had polio and wore noisy silver braces. Consequently, she was self-conscious and shy. I couldn't stand the noise those braces made and thought she was ugly because of them. I would push my desk against hers to keep her from getting up and out. I remember one time when I knew she had to go to the bathroom and I penned her in. She wasn't even able to say, "Could you move so I can get out?" The memory of being that mean, instead of compassionate, was so difficult for me, especially when we talked about disabilities.

Over time in this process, I've learned to be honest about who and what I am. Consequently, I have been able to delve deeper, open up, grow, and make allies. Shutting people out just keeps you from being able to peel back through all the layers of bias and misunderstanding.

At first, for me, self-esteem activities were the easiest to present to young children. I attributed my own low self-esteem to negative childhood experiences, so I took great pride in implementing a curriculum that encouraged positive self-esteem at the East L.A. College Campus Child Development Center, where I work. I particularly liked activities dealing with the self (skin tone, hair texture, body size), family, and respect for others.

There was a little girl in my class who had long beautiful hair that other children and adult visitors liked touching. I could tell she didn't like it and I knew we needed to talk about it so I decided to use one of our persona dolls, Marisela. Marisela had very long and curly hair. I introduced her to the children at group time and explained how she did not like the feeling of being startled when someone suddenly touched her hair from behind. She said she understood that she had long hair and that people were tempted to touch it but she would prefer if they would ask her permission to do so. Then I asked if anyone in our group had ever had that experience or a similar one. The little girl with long hair talked about similar feelings. Other children talked about their experiences, such as people touching an admired piece of clothing or a hair ornament. Finally, one child asked Marisela if she could touch her hair. The doll gave permission. Immediately, all the kids wanted to have a turn asking and touching. The last child who came up had a crew cut. He asked Marisela, "Can I touch your hair?" Marisela, of course, said yes. After he touched her hair, he looked at her face to face and asked, "Would you like to touch my hair?" I could sense that he had shared the same experience of people touching his almost bald head. I could see so many ways this experience of asking permission and being respectful had an impact on children's later interactions at the center. Experiences like this one encouraged me to use persona dolls to address issues of race, age, disabilities, and gender.

There was tremendous growth in each of the support group participants at the end of the first year and we unanimously voted to continue. Louise had been our facilitator, and she expressed that one of her goals was to see each of us move into that role. The second year would offer that opportunity. When we came back after that first summer, everyone opened up. From then on, people who thought they had an answer would jump into the discussion without looking at Louise for permission. And we relied on one another for support.

Sometimes I even brought things that happened in my personal life to the group for discussion and support. For example, one evening a friend and I were going to a concert and we met early to go to a little taco stand for dinner. She ordered her food and when I walked up to the counter the owner immediately said to me, "What do you want, mamacita?" My friend and I just looked at each other. We were flabbergasted. I really wanted to cry but instead I looked at him and said, "Excuse me, but my name is not mamacita and I don't appreciate you calling me that. You didn't make any reference to my friend's background." And he said, "Well, don't you think you're a little sensitive?" And I just said, "No, I'm a customer and I would appreciate it if you would just ask me what I would like to order, like you ask everybody else."

It hadn't been easy to speak up. The man was white and he was older. But I knew that I had to say something. After dinner we walked to the concert and the young man at the door said, "Good evening, girls." My friend Marcia and I just looked at each other and didn't say a thing. I think it was at that point I realized that there were different kinds of battles and sometimes I was going to have to choose which ones I wanted to address. That has been a real key for me. There are times when I say, "I'm going to deal with this one." There are times when I've let things go. And there are times when deep down I have a gut-level feeling that I should have addressed something and didn't.

For so long I had been hearing a voice in my head that told me, "Don't say anything. Don't say anything." I know now that I needed some key experiences to help me find my real voice, even if those experiences made me shaky and even if that voice of mine came out quivering.

I shared the experience with two people from my support group. Before that night I didn't really know that I had been developing my voice, but when I told them they both looked at me and said, "All right, Linda. You've got a voice. You've got a voice!" It was so exciting. For so long I had been hearing a voice in my head that told me, "Don't say anything. Don't say anything." I know now that I needed some key experiences to help me find my real voice, even if those experiences made me shaky and even if that voice of mine came out quivering.

We didn't talk much about homophobia during the first year of our anti-bias curriculum support group. Other "isms" had offered varying degrees of difficulty for each of us and we had plugged through them. I wasn't uncomfortable exploring or discussing homophobia in the group. My parents had taught me tolerance, and I had experienced racism. In addition, I had had experiences of working with gay and lesbian people, and so I had already worked through the discomfort that comes from not really knowing people. For example, in college I had worked in a record store and came in contact with gay men through the store. I remember one time some of us who worked in the store went out together to a drag show for which our boss had given us tickets. I was real naive back then, and I had no idea what we were going to. The owner's fiancée told me that we were going to a kind of play where there were just men and they played women's parts. "Oh, like Shakespeare in the old days," I said. The show was in the back room of a gay bar, and on our way in we had to go through the bar, which of course was full of gay men. Some of them were holding hands and making out. I immediately freaked! My friend calmed me down, saying, "You're okay. Nobody is going to hurt you." Can you imagine? Would I have freaked out in the presence of heterosexuals making out? Being exposed to gay and lesbian people in my everyday life through incidents like this one helped me learn to be open and grow.

By the time I joined the support group I had had friends and co-workers who were lesbian and gay, so I was less naive and more comfortable with lesbian and gay people. But I was uncomfortable talking about homophobia when I did anti-bias presentations. I found that when I listed the "isms" in our society, I would give a little description of racism, sexism, and so on, and then I would briefly refer to "lifestyle differences" without really talking about it at all. I think I was afraid of being confronted and challenged by someone with strong religious beliefs. And then, after one presentation, a young man approached me and said, "I've been to several presentations on anti-bias curriculum and it seems I always hear the term *lifestyle.*" Looking me straight in the eyes, this blonde-haired, blue-eyed, young man went on to say, "I am a gay man and I'm a good teacher. I work at a Christian school and if they knew I was gay, I think they would fire me. So it's really difficult for me when people talk about the importance and meaning of an anti-bias curriculum and they don't really talk about homosexuality."

I truly believe that nobody willingly puts himself or herself in a position to be discriminated against or hurt. And the more lesbian and gay friends I have, the more I see the agony they've gone through. It's just like people of color—this is a group of people that we have to stand up for.

Whew! There I was, a woman who as a young brown girl had not been validated. And I was failing to validate this man. I saw his hurt and his pain. I wanted to make it better for him so I tried to think of something to say.

"Should I go back and talk to the class?" I asked.

"No," he said, "They will only know it's me."

"You're right, and I apologize. It's not okay that I did not cover that 'ism.'" I went home and thought about it some more and took it back to our group.

We tried to deal with the issue together because it's a difficult one for a lot of people. Gradually it's become easier for me, though I'm still afraid of confrontations. Often I preface discussions by saying, "I know we each have our own beliefs and some of us have strong religious beliefs, however, I want to point out that we live in a society where more and more children in our classrooms will have two fathers or two mothers. I respect your beliefs and I'm not here to say what you have to accept or not accept, but it's really important to validate all children." Sometimes I will use myself as an example and explain what it was like to grow up not being validated. I've seen heads nodding and then it's easier to address.

I truly believe that nobody willingly puts himself or herself in a position to be discriminated against or hurt. And the more lesbian and gay friends I have, the more I see the agony they've gone through. It's just like people of color—this is a group of people that we have to stand up for.

Incorporating an anti-bias approach into the classroom also means creating an environment for families that is warm, inviting, comfortable, supportive, and sensitive, especially culturally sensitive. To me, creating this environment also means encouraging children and parents to speak up. There are a couple of stories about doing this that stand out in my mind. A couple of years ago, I had two siblings in my class who were primarily Spanish speakers. Like their mother, they were both shy and quiet. One day after the teaching assistant had finished passing the bowls of food for lunch, she noticed one of the siblings weeping quietly. He only spoke a few words of English and she wasn't able to determine what was wrong, so she called me over. When I approached the little boy, he began to sob loudly. I asked him, in Spanish, what was the matter. He said, "Yo quiero lonche." She had inadvertently skipped him when she passed the main dish. She apologized, and after that, we worked with him. He became able to say what he wanted, and we saw the changes in the way his whole body relaxed.

When his sister went on to kindergarten, she also remained in our after-school program. One day she told us that a little girl at her other school kept hitting her and that the teacher never saw it happen. We encouraged her to tell the girl to stop, and also to tell her teacher. But this little girl was very shy and though she tried, it didn't work. Next we talked to the mom and suggested that she talk to the teacher. She was reluctant but a few days later came in to thank us. She had gone to her daughter's teacher and told her that she really needed to take care of the situation. I congratulated her and told her I thought what she did was very difficult. About a week later I saw the little girl and she told me her classmate wasn't hitting her anymore. This story is important for the growth it shows in two generations.

Another Latino family in our program had two daughters, both of whom were light-skinned, blonde-haired, and had light-colored eyes. On the older girl's first day of school the staff oohed and aahed about the girls' looks. They made comments like, "Oh, your little girls are so pretty, they look like dolls!" and "Wow, they are lucky to have such gorgeous blond hair and blue eyes." The mother, who had darker skin and hair, beamed with pride. She said that people always thought the girls were white and sometimes questioned who their mother was or asked if she was their babysitter. She even talked about how life was going to be easier for them because they looked more like the dominant culture.

The family was at our center for a total of five years before the younger daughter graduated from the program. During this time, the mother became very interested in anti-bias curriculum. She also became aware of the preferential treatment her daughters got because of their good looks and light-colored skin, eyes, and hair. By the time the older child was in kindergarten, the mother had begun to notice how her daughter used her looks to get what she wanted. For example, she noticed that the teacher almost always chose her daughter to be the door monitor when the child assigned to the task was absent. She said she watched while several children raised their hands to have a turn, but her child was usually chosen after she raised her hand way up high, made cute little facial expressions, and yelled out, "Me, teacher. Me, teacher!"

The mom became so aware of the privileges her child received this way and so concerned about them that she said she was on a campaign to make sure her daughter didn't grow up thinking she could have whatever she wanted because of her looks. She told me about an event that took place during a morning carnival at the older daughter's school. All the children were given a cup of lemonade, and naturally, there were many children who wanted a second serving. They were told that their parents would have the opportunity to buy them another drink when they were picked up from school. At dismissal time, many children were asking their parents to buy them another lemonade. This child's mother said that she could not have another one, and the girl threw a tantrum. The woman selling the lemonade looked at the child and said, "Since you are so pretty, I am going to give you another cup."

"If I hadn't had this anti-bias training at your school," the mother told me, "I would have been so proud. Out of all those kids who wanted more, this woman was picking my daughter. Instead, I knew that what she was doing wasn't fair. I knew that she was picking my daughter because she was light-skinned, pretty, and blonde. So when she handed my daughter the lemonade, I said, 'No, thank you.' Of course, my daughter was really angry about that. At home I explained to her that the woman had singled her out because she was pretty and that wasn't fair to all the other children. And I asked her how she would feel if another child was the only one offered a free drink because of her looks." Now this parent is taking courses in early childhood at Cal State and calls us to ask for help with anti-bias activity ideas to use in her curriculum courses.

I feel that I have become a better teacher through my training in anti-bias education. When I first started teaching, there was a warmth about me. Parents responded to that warmth and could see that I respected their children. They told me I was a good teacher, but I didn't feel it was true. I still felt this sense of needing to emerge—knowing that I wanted to blossom, but not being able to open up. Anti-bias work helped me to get in touch with myself and reclaim my culture. That gave me confidence, and so I developed into a better teacher. And finally, I can say, "I am a good teacher."

But in diversity work there is always room for more growth and training. I applied and was accepted for the California Association for the Education of Young Children's Leadership in Diversity Training. It consisted of three one-week training sessions followed by a year of follow-up work and presenting workshops. I continued to explore my biases in this training. At first it was so difficult that at times I didn't want to continue. I came to understand that when I felt like quitting anti-bias work it was because I didn't want to experience any more pain. But I did continue, and I learned so much, not only about racism and oppression, but especially about internalized oppression. I was able to understand why people of color buy into the dominant culture. I began to realize that I didn't have to be so hard on my own people for wanting to be white. I came to understand that we all do things for reasons, and we need to understand those reasons.

I also learned how I can be biased about white people, too, even though I don't have the societal power behind me to back up those biases. Sometimes I think that people will be prejudiced just because they're white. Sometimes I'll say that someone is "too white," which means that I think they will be prejudiced, even if I don't know them. For example, when I first met my good friend Julie, who is white and fifteen years younger than I am, she was Louise's assistant in the anti-bias support group. For the first year, her job was to take notes, and I dismissed her as this young white girl who always talked so fast. Then in the second year she became a participant in the project, and through our conversations and through doing a workshop together, I came to realize that she was really aware of white privilege. She would always say, "You go first, you're the person of color." It's so easy for me to always take the back seat, because of internalized oppression, and Julie really pushed me to take the lead. She is one of my closest friends and one of my strongest supports in doing anti-bias work, and I almost missed out on that because of my assumptions about her.

As threatened as I might feel, now I allow myself to inter-act with people and open up to them, even if I am hesitant. People have hardly ever failed to be pretty open and sensitive; I say that they failed my "too-white" test! Everybody has their own story. Consequently, I am really aware now of not label-ing people and not making assumptions about them.

I can remember a time during one of the trainings when I felt totally incompetent. I felt that I could not understand any of the material; I felt stupid and incapable of under-standing what I read. Phyllis Brady, one of the trainers, noticed that something was wrong and asked me if I wanted to go outside to talk about it. Immediately I began to cry uncontrollably and confessed what I was feeling. We sat on the grass and she let me cry while she gently placed her hand on my arm. I cried for a long time. Then she asked me to try to get in touch with any experience that was bringing up these feelings. Suddenly I was in my first-grade class. We were all making hats and needed to follow the teacher's verbal directions. I had lost a step and couldn't bring myself to raise my hand and ask for help, so I began to cry. I remembered feeling so stupid, and Phyllis said, "You know Linda, you were not stupid. You just weren't able to ask the teacher for help. It was okay not to understand."

Something in that process of talking to Phyllis made me realize that I was capable of understanding, that I did have a voice, that I could pick up a book and understand what I was reading. It also helped me realize that I can ask questions and feel comfortable with people who I have labeled as smart.

Over the years of my journey, a new world opened up—partly because of my anti-bias work and partly because of my participation in the Women's International League of Peace and Freedom (WILPF), the oldest international women's peace organization. The Los Angeles branch of WILPF sponsors a yearly Children's Peace Camp. The first year that my daughter attended the camp, I decided to stay for a couple of hours just to check it out. Those two hours turned into a week and eventually into a yearly commitment. I was hooked on the Peace Camp because I saw how the teacher, Kay Taus, combined anti-bias curriculum and peace education to create an environment where children would learn about themselves and others, think critically, and learn how to take action and become peace activists. The underlying theme was respect for others. The camp experience was a positive one not only for the campers, but also for the adults who volunteered.

The following year I joined the camp planning committee. By the third year, I felt ready to attend one of WILPF's monthly meetings. I really enjoyed my first meeting. Most of the women in the Los Angeles branch of WILPF were about sixty years old, and many were older. One was nearing her hundredth birthday! Most of them were Jewish. I immediately sensed that these women were strong, determined, committed, and often feisty peace activists. Since that first meeting, I have learned so many things from my "WILPF sisters" herstories and experience, especially to always have hope and never to give up. Each year WILPF holds an International Women's Day luncheon, which is now a tradition for Amanda and me. The first time we attended the speaker was so dynamic that my fourth-grade daughter said, "Sign me up. I really like this." Sometimes she complains about my involvement, but every time I take her, she says, "Sign me up again." That always helps me keep going.

I am currently a board member of our branch. I have attended leadership trainings and have participated in a couple of their national congresses. At my first leadership training in Philadelphia a few years ago, I met Roberta Spivek, the editor of the WILPF magazine, *Peace and Freedom*. She had read my application for the leadership institute and wanted to know more about anti-bias curriculum. She asked me to write an article about it for *Peace and Freedom*. Writing scares me to death so, reluctantly, I said I'd think about it. Over the next year she kept calling and offering encouragement. Finally, I said okay. And from writing that article, I saw how things really do come full circle. Louise Derman-Sparks' mother is a member of WILPF, and when Louise went back East to visit, her mother had a copy of the magazine on her coffee table. She had read the article, and she said, "Oh Louise, so this is what you do." And then Louise came to me and said, "Thank you, Linda. You validated me." It made me think all the way back to that first parent meeting about anti-bias curriculum at Pacific Oaks and how Louise's presentation about anti-bias work had made me feel like my experience was validated. Finally, I got to return the favor!

So WILPF and the anti-bias curriculum support group have worked together to make me stronger. And now I see that this growth is an ongoing process, and a slow one. I know that it doesn't end, that I'm still growing, and I'll keep growing forever. For example, as a member of the support group, I was excited about doing the activities, but I didn't feel like I was able to train others. With experience, I'm gaining the confidence I need to be a trainer, to allow people to go through the process themselves, and to be comfortable not knowing it all.

I have also seen changes in how my family thinks or reacts to some of the issues I'm involved in. At first when I got involved in this work, my whole family questioned what I was doing: "Why do you make everything a race thing? Why don't you just let it be?" But along the way, as I shared what was happening with Amanda, I think they became interested in it and excited about it too.

My father has become a real support for me. I used to get angry at him because he wouldn't take a stand or question the way things were done. I see now that this is because he was taught not to cause waves. Now he listens quietly when I talk to him about different issues and then gets excited and tells me how I've got to change this or that in the world. He's gone to one or two WILPF meetings with me, and he has shared a lot of his experiences. Now I empathize with him because I realize what he's gone through. It's so painful to hear him talk about not getting to participate in a spelling bee—something he was really good at—because he was Mexican. There were times when I would forget who I was because I wanted to be white and fit in. My father has never forgotten who he is.

There is also a scary part to this work—losing friends. It seems that sometimes as you start becoming more verbal and standing up for yourself, friendships can start collapsing. I had a friend tell me I was becoming too powerful. She didn't understand, and when that happens, it's a real loss. It's been happening to me for two or three years now, so at this point I just have to let go.

I have finally reached the point of knowing that what I have to say is important and how I say it is fine. By accepting that this work is part of me, I don't have to hold back.

And there are times when doing this work is overwhelming, so I remember to choose my battles—knowing that I can't save the whole world, but I can contribute. I know I still need more training, and I need to keep connecting with other people who are doing anti-bias work. But I have a sense of freedom now. Rather than feeling intimidated or inferior, I plunge in and tackle some issues.

There have been so many joyful moments—meeting so many good people, being able to stand up in front of people and talk, not letting my accent or mispronunciation of words silence me. I have finally reached the point of knowing that what I have to say is important and how I say it is fine. By accepting that this work is part of me, I don't have to hold back.

I don't think there are any shortcuts. People have to be open and go through difficult times and experiences. I know this now and have come to admire everyone who does this work, whether they are people of color or white.

One of the most exciting things in my life is having my daughter. Amanda was empowered at a very young age.

Because she was at Pacific Oaks when they were developing the anti-bias curriculum, she really soaked it up. She and I both learned to think critically about issues of bias at the same time, even though she was four and I was thirty-four. I hope she will continue this work. She has developed her voice at her young age—a voice to help ask the important questions: How can we implement our work? How can we make teachers aware? How do we train people? How can we get this going at all levels? The process is slow. But I believe that if we start with young children and continue throughout their education, we will have a society of individuals who care.

Discussion Questions

1. Linda writes about the many ways her family is a key part of her anti-bias thinking. What roles does your family play in your anti-bias journey?

2. How do you think Linda's experience as a speaker of a language other than English shaped the way she approaches her anti-bias work? How does your experience with language shape your development as a teacher?

3. Linda uses the term *looksism* to describe how people are influenced by popular and stereotypic images and judge others by their physical characteristics. Think about your reactions to people you are meeting for the first time or people you see on the street or in stores. How are your reactions shaped by the way people look? What stereotypes do these reactions reflect? How do these reactions affect your relationships with co-workers, parents, and children?

LaVita Burnley

Staying True to Myself

I am an African American woman with a colorful mixture
of cultures within me. My family lineage goes in many
different directions. My grandparents on both sides are of
African American descent. My mother's heritage is African
American, West Indian, and Blackfoot Native American. On
my father's side, I also have French heritage from my great-
grandmother, who was white. There was a lot of secrecy about
this blended heritage when I was a child, and in particular, a
lot of silence about my father's half-French biracial mother.
She died very young from tuberculosis, which has made it difficult to learn the history of her people. Her mother (my great-
grandmother) had always been described to me as a very, very,
fair-skinned woman, but the truth is that she was a white
woman in a time when the notion of "mulatto" children was
not accepted. So there was a lot of shame about my grandmother, and for years nobody in the family wanted to talk
about her. As children, my cousins and I could see that there
were differences in our family, different hues in our faces and
in old photographs of our relatives. As we grew up we often
poked fun at how fair-skinned many of us were, but we didn't
really ever ask why. We were told that our family was just very
fair-skinned. It was unthinkable for us to ever ask if grandma
was a white woman! It still is an issue that is not discussed or
mentioned around the elders in my family.

This silence about our blended heritage made me more hungry for answers about my family. Just recently I went to see my cousin, and he's the one who gave me more information about our family's history. He had done research on our family tree and had traced our lineage back to the Huguenots who emigrated to the Carolinas in 1736. It was at that moment that I began to feel a real connection to my family's past. I also talked to my last surviving uncle from that family, and to my Aunt Catherine, who had helped to raise me and my younger brother when we were very small, and she told me the whole story about my great-grandmother. It was like another piece of the puzzle falling into place—I could feel my whole body relax. I had felt so disconnected from my own family's history, like I didn't know who I was or where I came from. And it made me even more determined to avoid this secrecy with my own children. I believe that if you know the past, you can guide the future. I want to be able to sit down with my children and tell them where they come from, who their family is. I don't want to harbor that shame or that secrecy. I don't want my children to spend a lifetime guessing.

My mother took out two bags, one brown and one white. Then she told me, "There are some people who look only at the color of the outside of a bag and not at all the lovely things inside. Those same people will look at you and want you to look more like this white bag, without much color."

In my early childhood years, I lived in a middle-class suburb of Chicago. I was the child who integrated the preschool that my daughter now attends. And I vividly remember being four years old and running home a few days after I started school, telling my mom, "Guess what? Guess what? There's a colored girl in our classroom!" My mother, who was making dinner, dropped the spaghetti sauce all over the floor. I didn't know why she looked horrified and upset. I didn't understand why tears were streaming down her face. She picked me up and gave me a hug. And I said, "Mom, this is a good thing, isn't it?" When the teacher had made the announcement about the school's new colored girl and reminded everyone to be nice to her, I had no idea she was referring to me. I remained the only person of color at that center for the entire year.

My mother went to speak with the teachers about the incident, but they could not see the damage of singling out a four-year-old child about her race. Nonetheless, my parents kept me in that school for many reasons. One reason was to urge the town we lived in to make long overdue changes. I can also remember hearing my family talk about Martin Luther King marching in Chicago and how important it was for them to continue living in the area where we lived no matter what.

When I started kindergarten in that same town, I remember my mother talking with me about how some people were only going to look at my skin color and not all the other wonderful things about me. She took out two bags, one brown and one white. Then she told me, "There are some people who look only at the color of the outside of a bag and not at all the lovely things inside. Those same people will look at you and want you to look more like this white bag, without much color." I remember worrying that she would start crying again and wondering why she was talking about it right before school. In hindsight, I know she was trying to prepare me for all the pain and heartache that I might encounter at my new school.

My parents were divorced when I was seven, so for the first time in my life I wasn't able to share my thoughts about my struggles with both my mom and my dad. The year before we moved away from my father I had also lost a brother. My older brothers moved to their dad's home in Philadelphia and learned to cope with the loss in their own ways. To start fresh, my mom and my younger brother and I moved to southern California. Before, I had had a huge extended family. In California, I was in a foreign land, isolated from my family but surrounded by many different types of people. My mother immediately tried to fill the void for me. I took dance lessons, piano lessons, and joined a glee club.

When I was in junior high, we were living in South Central Los Angeles. Once again, the school in my neighborhood wasn't good, so my mother wanted me to join a voluntary bussing program. I would be bussed an hour and a half away to Patrick Henry Junior High in the San Fernando Valley. My mother and I discussed the idea, and I said I would try it for a year. There wasn't a lot of support for this in our community. Thinking of the long bus ride, the difficulties of going to an all-white school, and the isolation from other kids in the community, neighbors would say to my mother, "What are you thinking? Why would you do that to your daughter?" But she was determined to get me the best education I could possible have.

It was so difficult. As our bus pulled into the all-white town of Grenada Hills, the parking lot echoed with horrific name-calling from both parents and students. I remember wondering why the adults were so mad at a bunch of kids they did not know.

Throughout the year, I struggled with teachers pretending I was invisible in most of my classes. I would sit at my desk and wonder what gave them the right to mistreat me. At that fancy white school, they really hadn't taken the time to know that I was a good student, that I was trying hard to get a "good education," as I heard the mothers of my neighborhood say to their babies as they put them on the bus in the morning. One Chinese American teacher was a little more supportive. In hindsight, I think that she may have known firsthand what it was like to be the odd person out. When the other students would make fun of me, she would try to stop their crude remarks right away. In the majority of my classes, though, the

teacher would pretend not to hear. Health class was the worst. There were three other students of color in that class, and the teacher refused to acknowledge our presence. We could raise our hands with the right answer, and he would never call on us, even when none of the white students in the class had the answer. It was like we didn't exist.

And there wasn't anyone to talk to about how awful it really was. Those of us who were being bussed didn't necessarily live in the same neighborhood. We didn't talk to one another on the bus to or from school—we were all just trying to get through it. I couldn't tell my mom, either. She wanted me to get the best possible grades. She'd say to me, "You do well. Don't you come home with a C." I didn't know how to tell her what was going on in that school, especially given the pressure she was getting from the community about the decision to bus me in the first place. And I had promised her that I would try.

The year went by slowly and painfully. At the end, when I received my report card, it was obvious that my health grade was a mistake. I had gotten only As and Bs on every report or exam, and yet there was a C on my report card. When I approached the teacher, he looked me right in the eyes and said, "I have never and I will never give a black a grade higher than a C." Instantly I became numb and speechless. My white classmates made fun of me as I walked back to my desk. How was I going to tell my mother?

I had to show her my report card, and I knew I was going to get it. "LaVita," she said, "help me understand why you got this grade." When I told her everything, she was furious. She called the teacher and set up a time to meet with him. He didn't show up for the meeting. Finally, she got him on the phone again, and he said to her, "I don't know why you people push this issue." After that, my mother went to the office and talked with the principal and the teacher. It was never discussed again, and I never returned to Patrick Henry.

When I look back, the most difficult thing about that experience was that I did not understand his reason. How could this be? Why was I waking up at 4:30 each morning to be at that bus stop by 5:30, only to have a teacher treat me so badly? Was this getting a good education? None of it made much sense to me.

As a result of my experience at Patrick Henry, my mother packed us up and moved us to Hollywood a month later. We lived in a much smaller apartment, but I went to LeConte Junior High School. It educated children from all over the world. In her quest for a school that believed in equitable education for all children, my mother practically interviewed the principal. This was embarrassing for me at the time because she seemed so cold and hard, and she asked pointed questions like, "What is your policy on inclusion?" She also shared with the principal my past experience at Patrick Henry, and she was assured that LeConte would be different.

LeConte was difficult for me at first because I had to adjust to another new environment where there were very few people like me. But the school orientation was pleasant and completely different from my prior experiences. I had classmates from twenty-six different countries, and I often wondered if their parents were on the same mission as my mother. The issue of race came up when a young man of European descent wanted to date me. His parents felt there were many nice white girls that he could spend time with and encouraged him to cease his friendship with me right away. My friend and I agreed that our love would conquer all, but I remember feeling those same sick feelings that I had grown accustomed to at Patrick Henry, as if I was uncomfortable in my own skin.

When I graduated from high school I felt the world was mine for the taking. I wanted to go to college and find a career that paid a lot of cash! I was blessed with an opportunity to surround myself with friends who cared a great deal about my future. I landed a well-paying job with a huge supermarket chain. I worked hard and went to school in the mornings. I advanced in every position and was promoted twice. I was nineteen and solely interested in making money and living for the moment. In the circles in which I traveled, my skin color really did not matter. It mattered that I had the "green" to spend.

After five years of this lifestyle, I discovered that I was very lost. I didn't realize it until I was invited to a family wedding in Chicago. I attended the wedding and found the warm and loving extended family I had left when I was seven, a family that was struggling with its own identity, with this secret of

At the end, when I received my report card, it was obvious that my health grade was a mistake. I had gotten only As and Bs on every report or exam, and yet there was a C on my report card. When I approached the teacher, he looked me right in the eyes and said, "I have never and I will never give a black a grade higher than a C."

"mixed blood" running through our bodies and no one ever talking about it openly. I met people who knew me in my infancy and discovered that, although I had been gone for most of my childhood, they had held on to me in another way. They had documented my early years. They knew when I learned to ride a bike and who my favorite uncle had been. They looked like me and had my mannerisms. For the first time in years, I felt like I had family. It felt like rediscovering myself.

As a result of my trip to Chicago, I considered returning to where I was born, to my extended family, to Evanston, Illinois. I had fallen in love with the beautiful yellow and ruby red leaves the fall brings the Midwest and the thought of getting to know my father's family. I challenged myself, at twenty-two years old, to face those family realities. I decided that it wasn't enough to count cash, spend numerous hours under the sun, and wait to see what would happen next in my life as a Hollywood resident. My journey across the country began with me explaining to my mother my need to find something that made me feel complete. I had no idea what it would be, I only knew I had to find it soon. I relocated in early winter with a heart full of "dreams deferred." I knew exactly where I wanted to live and where I thought I would feel comfortable. I wanted to live in Evanston, a college town, and go to school. I wanted to surround myself with a loving and supportive family. I believed in dreaming big.

My first winter was the most difficult. My little Fiat Spider barely survived the drive across the country, and then a severe cold snap did it in. It needed parts that would take months to arrive, so I got rid of it and started immersing myself in the culture of the area, using public transportation to get myself around. Shortly after my car died, I was fortunate to be steered in the direction of a job. A cousin, understanding my need to make a difference in the lives of people, suggested that I work with young children. I was willing to give it a shot and thought at least I'd learn something. I interviewed for a part-time position at a local preschool. I had taken some classes in child psychology and social work so I spoke some of the lingo. I attended a local university in the mornings and was an assistant teacher in the afternoon.

I received a promotion shortly after I started because I was able to communicate well with the teen mothers during the intake process. I had my own classroom and spent a great deal of time conversing with the young mothers about their issues. I believed this was an extremely important piece in building day-to-day trusting relationships. I grabbed every opportunity to teach them ways to become critical thinkers. We spent time discussing money management, resource and referrals, and effective ways to be heard by their own parents. I enjoyed the work and was beginning to explore my faith. I felt spiritually full and had a purpose that made me soar in areas I had no idea I could reach. The work was rewarding, and the most ironic thing was that it paid pennies!

The community we served was diverse economically, ethnically, racially, and by religious affiliation and family make-up. Half the families had their child care tuition subsidized through the Federal Title XX program. These families were all people of color, mostly Latino and African American. Many of them were teen moms, and of course, to qualify for the subsidy, all of them were poor.

It was important to me, that first year, to learn a way to be respectful of all of the family styles and to be sensitive to cultural differences. Many of us young and impressionable teachers were looking for reliable mentors with defined mission statements. I began reading any book I could find that talked about cultural differences. The first one I found to be extremely helpful was *Anti-Bias Curriculum: Tools for Empowering Young Children.* It provided me with hands-on activities to do directly with the children, especially when I helped them explore their differences. But the more I expressed the need to celebrate these differences, the more isolated I felt.

I began to realize that the program where I worked offered an anti-bias/multicultural curriculum, but it could not maintain an equitable environment for the parents and the staff. We had all the developmentally appropriate practices, and we thought that we followed the anti-bias philosophy well. As a staff we were divided— African American, Jamaican Americans, Belizeans, and European Americans. We were all struggling to believe in the anti-bias/multicultural curriculum that was put before us and which we were made to follow. But we had trouble with our own biases, which were never discussed. The European Americans seemed steeped in the belief that we were all the same. This was the time in my life that I began to deal with the issue of my grandmother being French. I thought that if they knew that my great-grandmother was white, the very people who I sometimes detested would be shocked. I wondered if it would make a difference in their perception of me.

> *I thought that if they knew that my great-grandmother was white, the very people who I sometimes detested would be shocked. I wondered if it would make a difference in their perception of me.*

I began attending workshops and studying a variety of early childhood theorists. I developed my own mission statement after I had my first cocaine-addicted infant in my classroom. At first I was very angry with the parents of that baby, and judgmental. This young woman of color had children, something I wanted so badly, and she knew she had a drug problem, she knew what that meant for her child. I sat in the intake with her and thought, "How dare you? How could you have this chance to be a mother and do this to your baby?" I couldn't really listen to her. I couldn't really hear her story.

I had another child in my room whose parents were European American. The father was a professor and the mother was a housewife. They were very well off, but their child had severe fetal alcohol syndrome because the mom was an alcoholic. Several times she even came to pick up her baby when she had been drinking. At that point I saw that the disease of drug addiction and alcoholism crosses economic and racial lines. It wasn't just a secret in my community. That realization made me think about the drug-addicted young African American mom in a whole new light, and I was able to open up more, to listen to what they were telling me about their lives, to be there for those families in a different way. I felt ashamed of how judgmental I had been. I remember starting to understand the philosophy of seeing the family as a whole. I stopped being angry and opened up my heart. I learned to have a "teachable spirit."

By my third year at this center, I started to push the administration to make their practices more inclusive and to start with the relationships between the administration and the staff. These were important times for me to take a stand for what I believed in and not to get used to the status quo. The center was located on Chicago's wealthy North Shore, and our priorities were made clear for us. We held our allegiance with the full-fee families—the families who could afford to pay the full tuition—who, of course, were European American. It did not take me long to understand that this was a disservice to all of our children and families.

I made the choice to challenge every bone in my body and accept a position as a coteacher in a multi-age nursery school program in Winnetka, the second wealthiest suburb in Illinois and a homogeneously white community.

The center knew how to get their dollar's worth. The more subsidized children they could test out as delayed (no matter how small the delay), the more funding the center could receive. So every child whose tuition was subsidized through Title XX received a needs assessment, which included a battery of standardized testing. Whatever standardized developmental test you can imagine, those kids had to take. Of course, all these children were children of color, and many of them spoke languages other than English. The tests were culturally and linguistically inappropriate. As a result, some children would get labeled "delayed," which may have followed them all the way through school. At the same time, when teachers expressed concerns about a European American child who was clearly in need of evaluation, we were told, "Oh, his parents are both professors. There's no need to test him. Any developmental delays will be discovered as we go along." When I began to question these testing practices, I became unpopular with the administration.

I recall challenging the director of the center to look at her biases as they related to the African American parents and staff. Shortly after that, it became apparent to me that I would be a target for constant pin pushing. When I was told that I was burnt out and should seriously consider finding a new career altogether, I knew that I had to make a decision to go elsewhere.

I had a close friend who kept telling me about this great anti-bias/multicultural philosophy her center practiced and, more important, about the director who she felt lived it. By this time, it was hard for me to believe that a center on the North Shore could actually embrace such a concept. But I took my friend's word for it and interviewed for a position in Winnetka. The administration seemed to appreciate my straightforwardness and tried to assure me that this school worked diligently on those important issues. I realized for the first time in my career that there were European Americans who were trying to be accountable and who recognized issues of justice. Of course, I had read a great deal about others who had taken stands, but up to that point I had never honestly spoken face to face with a white person about these issues.

I made the choice to challenge every bone in my body and accept a position as a coteacher in a multi-age nursery school program in Winnetka, the second wealthiest suburb in Illinois and a homogeneously white community. This task was very different from anything I had ever dealt with. Because the community was so homogeneous, I stood out every place I went. When I went out during my lunch breaks, people would automatically assume I cleaned someone's house in the area or worked at that "day care center by the church." The only reason they didn't guess that I was a postal worker was because I wasn't in a uniform. The issue of race permeated the environment, and so did the issues of class and sexism.

The center was brand new, and it had been planned to reflect what the world actually looked like in terms of race and cultural differences that were not reflected in Winnetka. Anti-bias curriculum was to be at the core of the programming, and the director had handpicked a very diverse staff who she thought would buy into and practice an anti-bias approach. We came from all walks of life and we all had baggage to work through. Our director believed she had hired the cream of the crop to teach a community about anti-bias and multicultural early childhood practices. But then, in a staff meeting, she made the statement that all of us were racist and we needed to begin dealing with it now. I remember thinking, "This white woman has no idea what she is saying." I had taken a course on racism and learned early that I can be hateful and show signs of prejudice, but in this country, I can never be a racist. This is because my feelings do not affect the socioeconomics of any group. My people do not have power like that in this society yet. I later came to understand that this was her way of trying to jump-start a conversation among the staff. But instead, it made the European Americans feel angry and betrayed and the African Americans wonder if she was playing with a full deck.

By this time I had a sharp awareness and understanding of institutionalized racism, but I was not knowledgeable enough to begin to teach parents how to open up. This made it difficult for me to cope with the discomfort of the parents in the center, many of whom had never dealt openly with issues of race before. For example, one of my students became very fond of me and showed her affection by giving me hugs. This is surely not unusual in child care settings! Her mother, how-ever, became very uneasy when the child would greet me that way, and she would physically steer her in the direction of my white coteachers. One day she wasn't very successful at deflect-ing her, and so she remarked to me, "I would appreciate it if you would not hug my daughter." Then she asked the child, "Don't you remember what we talked about in the car?" I was shocked and angry. At the same time, I felt powerless and said nothing at all. I wanted to quit and go back to my community, but I refused. That would have been too easy.

So I developed a very thick skin to endure all the remarks and unspoken gestures. My biggest challenge was hearing children make negative comments about other races because that's what their mother or father said and it must be right. It took many sleepless nights before I was able to equip myself with the tools to defeat that battle. Most of all it took courage and patience. I wanted to prove to myself that I could endure until I made a difference.

The staff and director at the school agreed that the best way to help parents begin their anti-bias journeys was to infuse them with information—at open houses, parent meetings, and workshops. This was no easy feat. At parent meetings, where we would have a full house, the staff would address topics such as "Why Have an Anti-Bias Curriculum?" It always seemed to be my role to talk about the most difficult pieces because the three other African American women let it be known that they didn't want to speak. These issues were important enough to me, however. I wanted to get to the core of racism as it related to the teaching that was taking place with the students, even though I often felt like a target for parents who wanted to express their true feelings about a diverse group of people in leadership positions teaching their children.

One of the mothers told me, "I am a product of a biracial marriage and I have only been teaching my daughter about her European American culture, not her Filipino heritage. I buy only white dolls. We only stay within our safe lily-white town."

Of course, there were high points too. I will always remember one parent who approached me after a meeting. I could see that she was tearful, but she remained calm as she told me, "I am a product of a biracial marriage and I have only been teaching my daughter about her European American culture, not her Filipino heritage. I buy only white dolls. We only stay within our safe lily-white town." By this time tears were streaming down her face. We hugged and I realized for the first time that I was making a difference, helping someone begin a journey and recognize another side of herself. This opened a door and the parent continually reflected on situations with me. As a result, we became friends and have kept in touch over the years. Her daughter and I had a meaningful relationship too. More than a student/teacher relationship, we had a friendship!

It became known throughout the center that I was the key person to go to if you wanted to know honestly how the African American staff was weathering the storm. I would speak on

behalf of my "sisters" at all staff meetings, and I also had special times with the administration to challenge them to think about incidents that could be handled differently. For example, one parent refused to speak to the African American teacher in his child's classroom. This parent wouldn't leave his child with this teacher. He would look for a white teacher, instead. Also, he would speak to the white teacher's aide, leaving messages for the African American teacher in charge *while she was standing right there.* The aide would literally repeat his words to the teacher. This was a very awkward situation for everyone, and we allowed the behavior to continue for too long.

Although this was happening in another classroom, I heard the pain and the anger from the African American teachers who had grown accustomed to this terrible treatment. The teacher involved was very dark-skinned, and of course she didn't like being treated in such a disrespectful manner, but she would always say, "Oh, it's okay." It was very hard for her to stand up for herself because of internalized oppression she was experiencing. By this time, the founding director at the center had left. The board had hired someone to fill the position who didn't really understand or support the anti-bias approach. The director responded to this situation between the parent and the teacher by saying, "That parent just doesn't know how to relate to her. He thinks she's from a different stock." She also tried to say that it was just about class, as if mistreating someone because of their class is okay! I pointed out to her that through her inaction, she was silently saying that it was okay to mistreat a staff person for any reason. I often found myself advocating for others in this kind of situation because I could not believe that we were saying we were committed to the anti-bias philosophy and yet still had incidents like these occurring regularly.

And, of course, similar kinds of things happened to me at that center. For example, I recall being in the company of three wealthy white women who were discussing their vacation destinations. I was trying to keep most of my interactions with parents on a professional level. As the conversation went back and forth, I needed to interrupt to ask one of the parents a question about her child. When I did so, they all turned to me and, speaking in a high voice, one of them asked, "And what is Miss LaVita going to do with her vacation?" Everyone waited for my response. I began to answer, and one of the women interrupted to say, "We are going to Cancun for a week." The other women responded with congratulatory comments. I decided to try to push the envelope that day and get a word in edgewise, so I said, "I will spend two days in Puerto Rico and a week and a half in the Virgin Islands."

For a second or two their mouths just dropped open. Then their heads nodded with approval. "Oh," said one of the women, "That sounds wonderful. I spent time in such-and-such resort last year." I told her what a coincidence it was that I would be staying there too. From this ordinary conversation, I understood that the women in that circle simply did not expect me to have the same interests. It helped me understand that when people discover they are more alike than different, the flow of communication is easier. My relationship with women in their very affluent community moved on many different levels during my six-year tenure at the center. When I look back on similar incidents, I can see that as we open our hearts and take time to explore each other's worlds, our fears will be less of a burden to carry.

It took almost two years to get basic human respect at this center. Next, a time came when my ability to lead a program was being tested. At the end of those first two years, I remember looking back and realizing that I had been invisible at this center, but now I was setting the tone for what I believed was high-quality anti-bias curriculum. For example, I was determined to provide my students with experiences that showed people of color in a variety of roles. In Winnetka, most of the people of color that these white children saw were in service roles. At the local grocery stores, all of the clerks were African American or Latino, and the postal workers were mostly African

Americans. So I exposed children to interactions with people of color in power roles as opposed to the ones they were used to seeing. This idea blossomed into a center-wide approach and became a successful set of activities. For instance, we made sure that if we had an Officer Friendly speak with the children about safety, that person would be someone of color. We provided children with opportunities to explore, question, and react.

At the same time, many parents were dealing with their own issues of bias. I do believe most of them sincerely wanted their children to be respectful of all people. But to understand racism and to deal with its effect on young children, adults have to change lifelong behaviors that are difficult to shake. For example, parents might make racist comments at home about current events or television shows but then want and expect their children to behave differently at school. I had an ongoing conversation with parents about the fact that they were modeling one set of behaviors and expecting their children to act otherwise.

Then came the most intensely difficult experience of all my time in Winnetka. It remains painful and vivid in my mind. It was January of 1992, a day after Martin Luther King's birthday. I had taken the day off as a personal holiday and, when I returned the following day, I explained my absence to my students. This, for me, was going to be a perfect "teachable moment." I prepared a lesson on values, courage, and nonviolence. As a good early childhood teacher knows, you can't teach young children history, but I felt it was very appropriate to discuss the importance of Martin Luther King's contribution to the United States. A student teacher visiting from one of the local universities was sitting in on the discussion primarily because she was learning about the anti-bias curriculum in her class and had heard from her instructor that our school was the best at implementation.

I read a picture book of King's early years and then gave the children an opportunity to ask questions or respond to what they heard. I talked about the values that we shared with King in our classroom. Well, the activity spun off in an unexpected direction when I asked the children how they would feel if we had children of my color come to our school. One child immediately said, "I would not like it at all. My daddy says he has to lock up all the bad black people in jail."

That statement almost made me faint. I was totally shocked. Here I had been working with this same group of children for over a year on these very issues and they had not understood the message I thought I had brought forth. I asked if they knew I was the same color as the children in the book, and they said, "Yes, but you're the good kind."

Now the student teacher was frantically writing down every remark that she heard. I guided the conversation in another direction, hoping I could redeem my students, but it only got worse. The children started saying that they never wanted to have black kids as friends because they are bad and they should not be in their classrooms at all. I asked the child who was the most vocal, "If I have a little boy someday, wouldn't you like to play blocks or do waterplay with him?" He said no.

> *The children started saying that they never wanted to have black kids as friends because they are bad and they should not be in their classrooms at all. I asked the child who was the most vocal, "If I have a little boy someday, wouldn't you like to play blocks or do waterplay with him?" He said no.*

The student teacher who observed the activities took her notes to our center director, not believing that something like this would happen at a program that is known for its anti-bias work. The director reacted before she took the time to think things through, telling me that it was best for me to talk to parents about what had happened in a meeting within the next day or so. I was in so much pain that I was numb from the whole ordeal. I barely wanted to return to the school at all. Meanwhile, when parents heard this story they were outraged. First, that I would teach the children anything about Martin Luther King because it was history, and second, that I was saying their children were prejudiced.

The director remained insistent and we had a heated discussion. It took everything I had inside of me to return to school. Upon arriving the next day, she let me know that she had written a letter telling parents about the incident and announcing that we would have a meeting the following week. Then she tried to get me to agree to be there. We argued back and forth, and I was in such disbelief that I could not feel anything at all. I had to think about whether I would actually show up or not.

After a few days, the director came back to me and let me know how sorry she was for trying to push her feelings on me. She talked with some colleagues who did racism training, and she learned where she had gone wrong. She told me, "I have pushed that white-woman power on you, saying I am the boss and you will do as I say." Nonetheless, she had already informed the parents and scheduled a meeting. There wasn't any way to cancel or reschedule it without parents feeling like we were evading the issue. Though I considered staying home, I had to ask myself what the parents would think if I did. Perhaps they'd think I felt guilty or ashamed, or that I thought I had done something wrong, when in fact I was proud of what I had done, though horrified at the depth of bias it had revealed in the children. I didn't want to give them the opportunity to convict me in absentia.

The parent meeting was attended by parents, board members, and a few staff members who were there to support me. We were asked to walk into this room and each pick up a wooden building block. Then, as we placed our block on the table, we were supposed to state one value that was important to our own family. Each of us picked up a different-shaped block and added it to the structure we were forming. Some of the values people named were self-respect, hard work, love, and obedience. One of the words that stuck out in my head was commitment.

After everyone was seated, the director very eloquently explained what had happened in my class, using words that everyone could understand. But parents began to get very angry. They said, "No way. My child would never say that." "I know LaVita had something to do with changing their words around." "Why would LaVita teach four and five year olds that stuff anyway? That's not a part of the curriculum and we know it." "We need to stop this nonsense," one parent remarked, jumping out of his seat in anger. "This anti-bias stuff needs to be stopped at this center." Another parent who held a very high position in the court system stood up and said, "I know my son did not say anything like what you're saying he said. I marched in the sixties right along with those people. I did what I could. Yes, I do lock all bad people up where they belong." He concluded by saying that he felt that topics like Martin Luther King should not be discussed at all because they were very inappropriate. And he wanted everyone to stop putting words in his son's mouth. There were some parents who stood up and said, "Wait a minute. You have it all wrong. Let me help you understand the importance of your child dealing with this now instead of later in life when he discovers there is a world out there filled with all types of people and causes," but they were outnumbered and outshouted.

I sat and listened to these comments and could not believe it. I thought we had come so far, but we hadn't moved an inch. Parents whom I felt somewhat connected to had turned their backs on me. It was indeed like a public lynching. By this time my heart was pounding and I was in tears. The meeting went on and on. After forty-five minutes of this, I could not stand it anymore and decided to leave. I excused myself and let the white people work on their issues by themselves.

I carried my disappointment for a very long time. Many parents stopped talking to me, and some could not even look at me because of the way they had reacted as a group. I kept my chin up and continued business as usual. I found that I was really only working on my own biases toward them. I learned that when you begin to digest the anti-bias/multicultural philosophy, you are forced to learn to cope with others who have not begun to heal. I was ashamed at many of the thoughts that crossed my mind from time to time. But the children loved me just the same. After all, I was one of the "good ones." The scars from this experience lasted until I resigned from the school four years later.

A few years after that I heard this story from a parent. She reminded me how we would teach children to sing Happy Birthday in sign language. One evening her family was out having dinner at a posh restaurant. It was a grandparent's birthday, so both of the children stood up and started signing the birthday song. The father was very embarrassed and could not get them to stop. The mother, on the other hand, found this particular piece of our anti-bias education extremely important and meaningful. It became a family struggle between the values the father wanted them to have and the mother's way of looking at people and life in general.

During those years on Chicago's wealthy North Shore, I learned so many things about people who live in big homes with white picket fences—perfect nuclear families with enough money and resources to live very comfortably. The most important lesson was understanding the barriers that our society puts up when we are forced to intermingle with those different from ourselves. Fear stops us from being real with one another and keeps us from learning that we have common denominators when it comes to the education and well being of our children, regardless of the package we live in.

When I accepted the position in Winnetka, many of my African American colleagues felt that I had sold out, abandoned a population of children who needed me. One friend seized every opportunity she got to remind me that my hard work would continue to go unnoticed because "those people" didn't respect me as a professional. My professional friends in the same field who worked in the inner city reminded me that they were on the "front line" every day and I seemed to have forgotten the needs of children of color. This upset me until I started observing the children and families I worked with closely. I discovered that this group of families had needs that were just as monumental as the children in the inner city, if not more so. I say this because, from experience, I know that the children in the inner city are equipped early in life with tools for survival. Most families teach their children ways to constructively get around many limits—how to go to the corner store to purchase a few groceries with little money, who to look out for, and so on. The children in my center had another set of rules all together—mostly, they were handled with kid gloves, handed opportunities, and given the notion that they were superior. There was no need for them to learn how to survive in a world that was anything but accommodating. However, Winnetka had many teenagers suffering from eating disorders, contemplating suicide, and strung out on cocaine. The drug problem there was just as bad as at any inner city school.

I understood that the two populations would eventually meet up in life and what a rude awakening many of the children I taught were going to have, learning that the world was not all theirs for the taking. I had seen other white children and adults go through the same thing. When they found out that they were not at the center of the world, not the be-all and end-all, they had nothing to fall back on. They didn't know who they were or how to be in the world without all that privilege and power. They didn't have a strong culture and community to say to them, "Okay, you're not the center of the universe, but you're okay anyway Here are all these things you *are*." They didn't know how to move out of the crisis caused by their identity being so much about privilege. So, as I thought through this, I was able to clearly identify the strengths and the weaknesses of both groups of children. I began to organize my thoughts and could come back to my friends with the reason for the work I was doing.

I also let it be known that I was capable of speaking publicly about doing anti-bias work in a homogeneous environment, and I was quickly asked to speak at local directors' meetings, NAEYC conferences, the 1993 World Parliament of Religions Conference, and at local universities and small organizations. As in the parent meetings at the center in Winnetka, it was always my part to address the critical issues when we did workshops. I remember feeling like such a heavy. My piece was the emotionally driven area of our workshop because I was informing others about my journey and sharing real-life experiences that would force listeners to think critically about their own behaviors and feelings.

When white children found out that they were not at the center of the world, not the be-all and end-all, they had nothing to fall back on. They didn't know who they were or how to be in the world without all that privilege and power.

One of the most memorable presentations I did was in Denver at a national conference for an organization that was in its early stages of development. For the first time in my professional life I could have easily become irate toward someone in the audience. I presented on the use of persona dolls in the early childhood classroom. You might think this would be an easy task; however, one of the women listening constantly made derogatory remarks about "black people" throughout my presentation. I tried hard not to react. I was in a room with twenty middle-aged white women, and it started to feel like I was having to defend the entire race of people into which I was born. Her last remark was the last straw. She asked me if she could come up and touch my hair because she had never been this close to a "black person" before, and she wondered what our hair felt like.

On that day, God was working overtime for me. I paused, took a deep breath, and said, "After my presentation, when I am finished, if it will help you on your journey, you can do so." The other women in the room were really embarrassed for her and looked startled that I could muster up that response to such a question. She did come up and touch my hair, and then she remarked, "Your hair feels like cotton—I thought it would be much different."

I could have crawled out of that room and never looked back. This was a national conference in the early 1990s and folks were still struggling with the way African Americans look in this country. I knew that day that I was really onto something if I could make someone feel that safe to ask me such a tasteless question. Afterwards, I was pretty numb and immediately went up to my hotel room and bawled my eyes out. I never let my copresenters or my colleagues know exactly how I felt. But that was also the day that I met Louise Derman-Sparks, a pioneer in the development of the anti-bias curriculum. We spoke only briefly, but I believed she might understand the feelings I was struggling with inside, being the only person of color in the room and then being personally attacked on top of it. After that, I soared on my journey. Speaking with Louise for that brief moment, I knew I was on my way.

She asked me if she could come up and touch my hair because she had never been this close to a "black person" before, and she wondered what our hair felt like.

Finally, however, I got worn down by the constant nature of the work in Winnetka and the lack of support. The program and the support really changed when the founding director left. The new director came from the same background as the parents and didn't really understand the anti-bias approach. My attitude toward the work I was doing in Winnetka changed. I began to agree with my friends, to think that I needed to do more work with people of color. I remember feverishly saying that I needed to give back to a community that would be responsive to me, that would respect me as a professional, that would give me my just due. I wanted to take everything I had learned in Winnetka and infuse it into my own community, where I would be working with lots of diverse children, not just rich white kids. I wanted children and families of color to benefit directly from all the lessons I had learned.

At that point an opportunity came up for me that was totally unlike what I had been doing. I was asked to apply for a job at the Ecumenical Child Care Network (ECCN), working with churches that housed child care programs and the programs themselves to create better relationships. Most of the churches and programs served communities of color. They were looking for a "relationship expert," and some people from ECCN had seen one of my workshops and thought I'd be good for the job.

I was the last person to be interviewed for the position as project director. There were twelve other candidates. Knowing that I had spent years isolated in a classroom setting, I was apprehensive about the interview and the competition of those twelve other people. I interviewed on Monday, and on Wednesday I was offered the job. The project was only for a year, because the job was grant-funded and they only had a year's funding. I took a step on the faith that had gotten me through all those years in Winnetka, and I took the job.

I still work for ECCN. I help churches and child care programs enhance their relationships and improve the quality of their overall programs. I help them develop mission statements that both can live by and include the concerns of both the child care programs and the churches. We also have a program to help centers housed in churches improve quality and get accredited, and we support emerging early childhood leaders who are people of color. I work with child care directors to improve their leadership skills and to help them have lasting effects on the infrastructure in the communities they serve. At ECCN, I have opportunities to challenge people about institutionalized racism, and they listen to me. CEOs in boardrooms ask me, "What do you think, LaVita?" and they really hear what I have to say.

The work that brave souls have done with anti-bias education and the journeys each of us are on are all unique. As classroom teachers, we try hard to use the appropriate language, be respectful of all genders, religions, cultures, and races. But the most difficult piece I found is knowing what my own issues are and where they stem from. Most of us carry the information that our own families have given us, whether it be helpful or not. Then we discover along the way that we have to accept some of the teachings of our elders and do away with some so we can begin to live honestly. The alternative to this is to continue to carry the baggage into our adulthood and have a life full of regrets.

As I have traveled through this life trying to live this philosophy that I want my students to practice, I was really working on my own issues. There was a time when people would tell a racist joke and I felt too uncomfortable to ask them to stop. I grew out of that and became very vocal about how I felt. This made others feel that I was uptight and no fun, so I gradually moved away from certain circles of friends. One friend remarked that I had turned into a different type of person. I knew I had to seek out people with the same outlook on life. I realized that I needed to continue to challenge myself, to think critically every step of the way. Everyone has an area in which they know they should work, but it is half the battle when you can admit that to yourself and move on from there.

When I was first asked to participate in this book, I eagerly awaited to relieve myself of all the answers I had never been asked to share. I was so anxious to get every bit of detail on paper. It was so important to me to include all the real emotions that you go through as you begin to discover yourself. By the end of the process, I realized that to record my journey in a way that would stimulate the minds of many was not enough. I needed to ask people reading this book to consider their own beginnings—and to know that there is no end. To know that my journey is unique and yet very similar to others is the key to many of my current success stories. And even though I am not in a classroom setting at this time in my life, I am still challenging myself and others to stay true to themselves and, if we do, I know the rest will come.

Discussion Questions

1. What feelings and thoughts arose in you as you read about LaVita's experiences with racism? Have you had similar experiences?

2. LaVita describes an experience in which the director of the center where she worked said, "We are all racists and we need to start dealing with that now." What do you think the director was trying to accomplish? Why didn't it work? How might you have responded if you had been present in that meeting?

3. LaVita writes about the struggles of being an aware person of color in an unsupportive environment. If you had been LaVita's co-worker, what might you have done to support her? How might you have tried to interrupt some of the hurtful acts she describes? If you were in her position, what might you want from co-workers who saw themselves as allies?

Eric Hoffman

Traveling with Friends

My family lived in my grandmother's house for my first six years, and lots of relatives lived with us or nearby. My uncle's bakery, my grandfather's butcher shop—everything was within a few blocks in the Squirrel Hill section of Pittsburgh. And though it was a very Jewish neighborhood, I didn't understand that until we moved out of the city and into the suburbs. Until then, I had just assumed the whole world looked like my world. So although being Jewish was a big part of my early identity, I wasn't really aware of it. I didn't feel a lot of discrimination in the suburbs, but I did have a sense of being different, a sense that others were curious about me as a Jew.

I went off to college in Boston in the late sixties to study math and science. I also had an interest in education—I thought a lot about the way it worked, what it was, and what it should be—so I took every opportunity to take education courses, and I did volunteer work with different ages of children. I found that I really enjoyed being with preschoolers, so during my last two years of college I volunteered in a child care center.

When I think about that center, I know that if I were there now, I would probably call the authorities to come check it out. There was a lot of shaming and smacking and very, very little respect for children, particularly for children who were different. I remember two Spanish-speaking children who were either ignored or treated as if they had a mental illness. Many race and gender problems weren't dealt with at all. Children would often use racial slurs and the staff would simply respond, "We don't say that. We're all friends here. We don't notice color."

Well, it was obvious that everybody did notice color. Most of the teaching aides were black, and all of the head teachers and administrators were white. There was so much tension between the two groups, so much pretending. I was treated politely probably because I was male and a college kid, but at the same time, I was asked to do lots of "boy" things. Plus, there were whispers about me being a "fag." I felt like an outsider in a bizarre system, with no ability to change it. Not that I had a clue about what I would do. I was just as confused as anyone.

There was a great deal of sincere searching and discussion going on about what education should be, what it did to children, what racism and sexism and equality were. And it all seemed so false when I thought about what was inside that day care center door.

I was left with lots of doubts about myself and the world. Though quite successful as a student in school, I came away feeling unsatisfied. Looking back, I see that these feelings came from both my own confusion about diversity and from the turmoil of the times. There was a great deal of sincere searching and discussion going on about what education should be, what it did to children, what racism and sexism and equality were. And it all seemed so false when I thought about what was inside that day care center door.

I knew that it didn't have to be the way it was. Hearing those children put one another down—that wasn't coming from them. It was more like they were channeling the tension from the surrounding adults. So even though my early experiences with children were not very positive, they helped cement in my mind a commitment to dealing with bias. And that commitment has helped me make it through all my teaching experiments around diversity, some of which were not very effective.

I left college with a degree in architecture and decided to work for a year in a Baltimore preschool before I went to grad school. Lucky for me! It was a really good school, a place that held deep respect for children and was built on a knowledge of child development. Even though the staff didn't talk about diversity issues much, the difference between how children treated one another there and the ways they had interacted in Boston was startling. It gave me a new vision of what early childhood education could be.

I never did make it to grad school. I worked at a number of centers in various positions: cook, teacher's aide, head teacher, and the teacher-director of a parent co-op for graduate student families at Ohio State University. That was another formative experience. Most of the families were foreign born. The children in my class were from thirteen different countries. A third didn't speak English. So I just threw myself into the middle to figure out what I was supposed to be doing. It's one of those experiences that I wish I could go back and do again, now that I've thought through a lot more issues around children's language and diversity. Though I certainly wasn't prepared for it at that time, I did learn a great deal about working with children and parents from different cultures.

For example, I remember one group of Korean families. The fathers were enrolled in the university, so the mothers participated in the center. They had no conception of American-style preschools and expected rows of desks and a nun running the school. Instead, what they got was an open classroom and me! I can't help smiling about it now. They looked at me and wondered where the teacher was, but they ended up being very supportive once they got used to my style. Because I was a man working with young children, they assumed that I was a university professor. And there I was, flying by the seat of my pants.

I went into child care with no early childhood education background, and I didn't start taking early childhood courses until I'd already been working for about eight years. I wasn't a bad teacher, but I didn't really know how to create curriculum, how to teach through concrete experiences that tap into and respect children's intelligence. I remember my disastrous lecture phase—talk, talk, talking about racism and sexism. After one of my lectures on gender, I overheard one child say to another, "Boys have penises and girls have vaginas and that's sexism." I had no idea that language can be powerful for young children when it describes their experience, but totally useless when it has no connection.

I was trying out a lot of different discipline techniques too. I found that many of them made my classroom more orderly, but they didn't seem to help children with their questions about gender and other differences, questions that kept popping up in their conflicts. So I was frustrated. And after thirteen years of teaching, I stopped. I was just burnt out. I worked in a woodworker's store for a couple of years. Being away from the classroom, though, made me realize how important working with young children was to me. Luckily, I moved to Santa Cruz and met other teachers who were interested in the same issues and who had gone through similar frustrating experiences. I began to feel that I wasn't alone.

Cabrillo College, our local community college in Santa Cruz, asked me to assist with some early childhood classes, including the introductory course. It was wonderful to have had thirteen years of experience and to sit in on a well-taught beginning child development course. I recommend it to all teachers! It put all of my experience into a framework. It helped me understand the theoretical parts of teaching and gave me a structure for doing diversity work that made sense.

After that, I went back to school for a year, which really renewed my energy. At the same time, I started working at the Cabrillo College Children's Center. That was ten years ago, and I've been there ever since. I'm the master teacher in the preschool lab. My classroom is used to train teachers. Most of the children's parents are students at the college. We have up to thirty children, ages three through five, and eight early childhood students at one time, so it's a busy place. Part of both the joy and the frustration of my work is that I plan lots of activities, but it's often the student teachers who carry them out. You never know how things will end up when you hand your ideas off to someone who hasn't had much experience.

At about the same time I started the job, I was introduced to *Anti-Bias Curriculum*, the book by Louise Derman-Sparks and the ABC Task Force. It was a kind of revelation just at the right time: I had developed a good sense of how children learn, I was experienced as a teacher, and I was starting to use a style of discipline and conflict resolution that helped children solve their own problems. The book and I clicked. Then I did a three-day workshop with Louise Derman-Sparks. There was lots of positive feedback, and it was so exciting to find something that gave me some hope.

Really, though, what pushed me to change the most was a group of four-year-old girls I had my first year at Cabrillo. They were totally into their own "gender curriculum"—fashion, makeup, being sexy, putting down one another's looks—stereotypes straight off the TV screen. They would turn their backs on me at circle time and exchange socks. Nobody could get them interested in anything else.

So I went to my favorite consultant—my wife, who is also a longtime teacher. She handed me two flannel board people and a bunch of clothing cutouts. She said, "Eric, if they're interested in clothes, talk about clothes." It's always helpful to have somebody who can point out your wrong turns. I was stuck in my opposition to the stereotypes, and I'd forgotten that these girls were just trying to make sense of their world.

I named the flannel board characters Juan and Marisol. The children were captivated. They dressed and undressed them and helped me make all kinds of fancy clothes for them. I thought, "Great, now I can get back to my curriculum plans." Well, that didn't happen. The children started asking questions about Juan and Marisol—who was in their family, where did they live, how did they get to school, what were they going to wear for Halloween. And then they had great debates answering their own questions. They were very passionate about their ideas, and sometimes it got out of hand. I had to learn how to control the discussion without losing their passion.

The children's questions made Juan and Marisol come alive. They became new members of our classroom. We made up lots of stories about them at circle time—nothing fancy, just what they had for breakfast or why Juan didn't want to come to school or the fight Marisol got into—and I realized that the children were telling me all about their own feelings and questions, especially about what it meant to them to be a girl or a boy.

For example, the children wanted to know Marisol and Juan's favorite colors. I asked my usual question, "What do you think?" They agreed pretty quickly that Marisol liked purple, but they couldn't decide for Juan. Later, one of the boys came up to me and quietly said, "He likes pink." So I made Juan a pink blanket and pink boots. When I showed the class, there was a huge debate—I even had to break up a few fistfights. "Juan can't wear pink boots. He's a boy."

Now when I hear a child say that, I have an urge to come back with, "No, you're wrong." But I've learned the hard way that it doesn't work. No four year old worth her salt is going to change her mind that way, unless it's out of fear. Instead, I've learned over time to say something like, "You believe that boys can't wear pink. Juan is a boy and he likes to wear pink boots. Isn't that interesting?" Then I just leave it at that. And perhaps the next day I'll wear my pink shirt.

In other words, I try to provide experiences that will sow the seeds of change. Then, sooner or later, children will incorporate those experiences into their thinking. I've learned it takes concrete experiences, time, and faith in their intelligence. In this case, three months later, a new child came into the class and said, "But Juan can't wear pink. He's a boy." And another boy who had been dogmatically anti-pink said, "Of course he can! Those are his favorite boots and he can wear anything he wants."

Another year I had a child who found out her mother was a preschool teacher. I was the only preschool teacher she had ever known, so she told her mother, "You can't be a preschool teacher, you're a girl." It was a great reminder to me that four year olds make grand generalizations all the time. That's their job. It's the way they learn. And my job is to provide experiences so their intelligence can take over. And, at the same time, to help their families understand how that learning process works, so they can be more accepting of some of the off-the-wall ideas their preschoolers come up with.

I try to provide experiences that will sow the seeds of change. Then, sooner or later, children will incorporate those experiences into their thinking. I've learned it takes concrete experiences, time, and faith in their intelligence.

Over the years I've developed many more flannel board characters, puppets, and dolls. And I'm constantly finding new ways to use them to bring up conflict and diversity issues, incorporating them into all parts of the day, not just circle time. For example, if I notice that more boys than girls are building with blocks, I'll bring a doll over to a group of children and ask: "Can Laticia sit here and watch you build with blocks? You know, building blocks is her favorite thing to do." It's become one of the cornerstones of my teaching style, helping children bring new characters to life, imagine what it's like to be them, and think about what it means to treat others fairly.

I've started using my characters to introduce curriculum that has more definite anti-bias goals. I find that I can expand on successful curriculum activities I've used before—I don't need to start from scratch. For instance, I've always incorporated sensory activities, such as color recognition, into my planning every year. The children (and my puppets and dolls) talk about the colors of their blankets and shoes and favorite foods, I put out color matching games, and we sing color songs. One year I had Juan say, "I can see the colors, but I can't tell what those pictures are about." That began several days of stories about Juan going to the eye doctor and getting glasses. I also talked about my own glasses. We did informal eye tests on all the children. We looked at other things that help people see—magnifying glasses, telescopes, binoculars.

> I've found that the biggest boost to self-esteem comes from children helping someone else, especially when they help correct something they feel is unfair.

Then I brought up another question: What do you think people do when they can't see? I brought in Braille books and a Braille typewriter, and I invited people into the classroom who use canes and dog guides. The children helped guide one another through obstacle courses, and they used child-sized canes that I made. On a walk around campus, the children discovered Braille on the doors, and I helped them think about why it was there. Then they found doors that didn't have Braille tags, and their response was immediate: "That's not fair. If someone's blind, they can't tell what room they're going in. We have to get new numbers and someone has to put them up." I found out how to get the tags made, but that turned out to be a long wait (they were stamped in brass), so I had some numbers made on paper and the children glued them onto the doors.

And the children felt great about themselves. There's so much talk about the need to raise self-esteem, but often it's limited to "look at me, I'm special" kinds of activities. There's certainly a place for that, but I've found that the biggest boost to self-esteem comes from children helping someone else, especially when they help correct something they feel is unfair. It doesn't have to be a big thing. I remember when the children discovered a hole in my puppet's shirt. I told them I would fix it, but two days later, I hadn't. They refused to let me continue with my activity: "No, that's not fair, you have to fix it now!" So we all marched into the storeroom to get the sewing kit, and they sat and watched me sew the patch. They were so pleased that they got an adult to do the right thing. Parents asked me about it for days: "Maria said she made you do something. She was so excited, but I couldn't understand what she was talking about. What in the world happened?"

O nce you start thinking about anti-bias issues and bringing them into the classroom, you continually confront new problems. Recently I've been struggling with how to handle young children's relations with media images. There are so many ways they are bombarded with misinformation, and I'm always amazed at how powerful the images are in their minds. I was once talking to children who were doing "Indian whoops" like they had seen on TV and in the movies. When I said that Native Americans didn't really make sounds that way, their reaction was so interesting. One child, a three year old, looked at me like I was from outer space, turned around, and started whooping again, totally ignoring what I had said. A five year old asked, "Then what sounds did they make?" He talked about the sounds people might use when they were hunting and got involved in his own project using this as a starting point. It was an entire personal curriculum that went on for weeks. And then there was the four year old who said that of course Indians whooped, she had seen it on TV. I tried to explain that the people on TV were actors who usually weren't *real* Native Americans. She turned to me and said, "But it was

a *real* TV." All I could think was, "Come back to me when you're five and I'll try again."

You just can't expect young children to sort out what's real and what isn't. And media images are presented so dramatically that sometimes they have a greater impact on children than children's own experiences. Compound that with the joy of sharing those images through play—Mortal Kombat, Cinderella, Pocahontas, Power Rangers. Watch children play and you see their struggle to understand what it means to be a man, a woman, a member of an ethnic group. You see them learning to solve problems in ways that are dysfunctional. And I remember, as a child, loving movies like Peter Pan—I wasn't aware that they were filled with stereotypes. I wish I had the power to keep all children from being exposed to these images.

But I don't, so instead I have to face the challenge of counter-acting media power.

Again, my flannel board characters helped in this effort. Using group storytelling, we reworked media images so the children could create their own heroic characters. For example, some children wanted the flannel board people to be Power Rangers. They made felt and paper costumes for them, then we pretended to go into a magic cave where we discovered all kinds of predicaments that needed to be solved. One time the characters were in a boat out on the ocean and one of their pets fell in. The children told me what they thought the characters should do, using whatever magical powers they could think of. After we solved each problem, the flannel board people came out of the cave and everybody applauded. We gave them medals, and there were some for the children to wear too. Over time we gradually moved away from a focus on Power Rangers to a focus on the children's own sense of power.

Our school has also taken the stand that adults can't introduce heavily advertised images into the classroom, even "cute" ones like Barney and Mickey Mouse. We can only follow the children's lead. In other words, we're restrictive with adults but let children use whatever is in their minds, as long as it's safe. School should be a place where children can get help working out some of these images.

It seems to me that teachers use these media characters because they're fun, familiar to most children, and easy. They are part of our shared culture, even though they teach commercialism, sexism, and other biases. They are easy in the same way that "tourist curriculum" is easy—you focus on cultural differences in song or food or clothing without an understandable, supporting context. I've done plenty of that, and it can be fun, but I don't think children learn much from it. It's much harder to balance similarities and differences while presenting them in a framework that stimulates children's thinking.

So I've been trying to approach cross-cultural learning from a different angle—trying to "down-size" it to a young child's perspective. One unit of culture preschoolers understand is the family, and I find they're interested in the similarities and differences between their family and those of their friends. So I don't present exotic activities that are supposed to teach about Japan or Brazil or being Cherokee. My main focus is that the activity comes from Tadashi's family or Florinda's uncle or James' sister.

I try to imagine a child walking into another child's home. What might she want to ask? "Who are these people? What do you call them? Where do you eat? What do you play with? Where is the bathroom? Where's your bed, and what color is your blanket?" Children relate to those kinds of questions, because it's what they do in their own family, and because they know some of the people involved. They can accept that families look different, and everyone can participate in the sharing. Plus, when I approach multiculturalism from this direction, there's less tendency for me to think that only people of color have a "culture," while us white folk just have regular lives.

I am lucky, because most of the Children's Center staff and the early childhood instructors at my work are committed to tackling diversity issues. I've worked with people who haven't wanted to bring up bias issues with children—they thought it was too dangerous. But at Cabrillo, the anti-bias approach is a great fit. As a staff, we try to set goals and maintain an ongoing discussion of particular diversity questions. And even when we blow it or we don't agree, we continue to work as a group. We can usually talk, listen, and respect one another's efforts. We know we have to work together. It's such a relief to know that if I'm out of ideas or if my focus is in another place, somebody else will carry the ball. The issues are not going to roll away and disappear. I won't have to start all over again.

Of course, we don't always know what we're getting ourselves into! Thinking about diversity and bias brings up hard questions. Each time I think we've answered one set of questions, a new batch pops up. And we're not always sure what we're doing is right. But I do know that, because of our discussions, we're doing a better job now than we were four years ago. For example, an issue for our program as a whole has been bilingualism. Our center has long been committed to reflecting the population of our county, which is primarily Anglo and Latino. Two years ago my coteacher, who is bicultural/bilingual, stated that she wanted the school to become bilingual. After some long discussions, everybody agreed that it would be a long-term goal. We were already working to bring more Latino families into the center, and we made hiring bilingual staff a priority. Of course, it wasn't that simple. English remained the primary language spoken by the staff, and many of the Spanish-speaking children dropped their Spanish within the first year. That's not what we wanted. While most of the families wanted their children to learn English, they didn't expect them to lose their home language.

Each time I think we've answered one set of questions, a new batch pops up. And we're not always sure what we're doing is right. But I do know that, because of our discussions, we're doing a better job now than we were four years ago.

It's such a complex issue. The child care staff and the early childhood instructors decided to set up a series of meetings on language acquisition and retention. Staff members brought in the research and theories to discuss, and we had some outside speakers. We discovered more and more places where we had to rethink our program—the way we hire people, the cultural assumptions we've made in setting up our environments, the way we structure our group times.

Snack time is a particularly good example of a part of our program that needed rethinking. Children eat in small groups with student teachers. In the past, we've tried to make sure each group was racially and culturally mixed. But I think that was primarily for the benefit of the white children, to help them feel comfortable with diversity (which, of course, is one of our goals for all the children). But the Spanish-speaking children, and children of color in general, weren't being encouraged to make connections with one another since they were always in the minority. We started creating Spanish-speaking snack groups so there could be times in the day when bicultural children were in a Spanish-speaking environment. We're also trying other groupings to help Spanish-speaking children discover one another. And they still get plenty of time in the mixed groupings that promote cross-cultural connections.

Our dialogue on language continues because we have so many unanswered questions and concerns: Would it be best for our Spanish-speaking children to be in a completely monolingual Spanish environment? Should we immerse children at this age in an English-speaking environment? If the children learn English, must they drop their Spanish? What does it mean to be a truly bilingual center? Right now we agree that we have to keep asking, experimenting, and struggling to do what's best.

Often our discussions move us from focusing on children's learning to looking at staff issues, which is probably not surprising, since the adult world is really the source of children's bias. For example, we've made great strides in getting a racially and ethnically diverse group of children in the center, but we don't have that diversity among the staff. We're pretty much a white institution. We have to ask, Why are people who might have the right skills discouraged or eliminated by our hiring process and job qualifications? Are most of the teachers we've trained and sent out to our community in the last twenty years white? Is our approach too Anglo-centered? Have the people who have left our staff not felt supported or accepted? Do we really want people who look different, but who think and act the same as we do? These are painful questions. We're all good-hearted people, but we can't fool ourselves by thinking we're beyond our own biases.

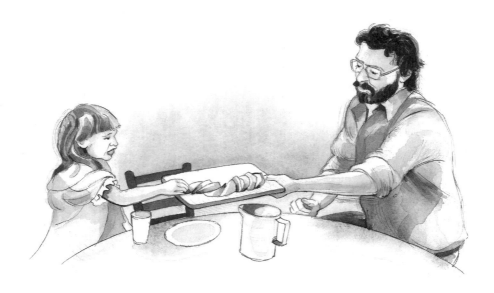

Or take gender roles. We're always looking at how boys and girls behave, how they're treated differently, how we can break down some of the separation. But what about the teachers? I'm a man in a traditionally female job. This affects my teaching, and I think it's valuable for everyone to be aware of the gender issues I'm confronted with. For example, how do I establish trust with parents, most of whom are women? I know that women learn to use body language, touch, and certain kinds of conversations with one another. It's not that every woman does it the same, but most important, it's generally interpreted in a positive way. Well, I don't use that style, partly because I'm not comfortable with it, and partly because the message is interpreted very differently when I do, especially with touch. So I've had to find other ways of communicating. It's not that my way is wrong or right, it's just a different way of being effective. I think we all do a better job when we are aware of those differences. The important thing is for me to notice and share this kind of information without getting into a "poor misunderstood me" or a "this is just the way men are" stance.

Then people feel free to talk about their own experiences, challenges, and insights.

Another issue under discussion is homophobia. Most of our staff agree that it's a bias we have to actively work against, but it's hard to get started when you know you'll get challenged or attacked for it at just the time you're least sure of yourself, least able to put into words what you're doing, and most likely to make mistakes. So I'm trying to clarify what's relevant to young children's lives, how to present our ideas to parents, and how to involve student teachers. What's interesting is that, on this issue, we've gone back to some of the beginning strategies people use in diversity work. We're mostly looking at the pictures on our walls and in the books we use to make sure we provide some images of gay and lesbian families. That's a good place to start, I think, as long as we keep going and keep finding ways to be more proactive.

But I do want to give children and adults some concrete experiences to contradict the demonization of gays and lesbians that's happening now. And as a bottom line, I won't allow anyone to give a child the message that her family is no good for her, that the love she feels for the people who care for her isn't right.

I don't mean I'm going to force parents or student teachers who are homophobic to change their opinion, any more than I could force preschoolers to change their minds. But I do want to give children and adults some concrete experiences to contradict the demonization of gays and lesbians that's happening now. And as a bottom line, I won't allow anyone to give a child the message that her family is no good for her, that the love she feels for the people who care for her isn't right. That would be totally unprofessional, and I have no problem demanding that teachers act professionally! Within the classroom, this isn't about discussing who has sex with whom, it's about accepting people who give love and support to one another in families and relationships, even when those relationships look different from mine.

I've had students drop my classes when I talk about homophobia. Some teachers I respect have a hard time with it too. Then I have to say to myself, "These are people whose work with children is wonderful. If I can't talk to them about tough issues, then I'm doomed, because these are my allies." So I just keep challenging lies as they pop up. I believe that some day this won't be such a big, painful issue. And I sure hope I see that day!

I see a lot of people in our culture getting very rigid about what they think should happen in families—very limited in the behavior they think is acceptable. I think there's a difference between being rigid and being clear. I'm trying to be clear about what the bottom line is for me. Solving problems without mutual respect is unacceptable to me. I want to be able to speak out when people with power use it in ways that dehumanize others. But respect can look different in someone else's culture or someone else's family, and lots of children grow up to be happy and healthy in families and schools that are unlike mine. I want to be flexible enough to recognize and accept those different ways, even if they're not my way.

To do that I've had to question my own assumptions. Take the issue of autonomy. In mainstream American culture, we want children to eat, sleep, toilet, climb, and read on their own as quickly as possible. It's one of the ways we try to be respectful, letting individuality and self-confidence blossom. In the past I was critical of families who helped their children "too much," who treated them "like babies." Now I'm seeing some of their actions in a different light—not as fostering overdependence, but as fostering relationship and interdependence. After all, those children learn to eat and toilet on their own, sooner or later.

In questioning some of my beliefs about independence, I'm realizing that some of the ways I've fostered it in the past may not have been as respectful as I had thought. When I refused to assist a child who wanted my help on a climbing structure, was I helping him master skills and increase his self-confidence, or was I creating doubt in his mind about his own ability to judge the safety of a situation? Was I creating doubts about the way his parents handle situations? Is that always respectful? These are the questions I'm now asking myself. I'm trying to get away from rigid rules, trying to assess each child and each situation. I want to be able to ask myself, "Is what I'm doing right now forming a trustful relationship and building this child's confidence?" That is a bottom line goal for me. I get different answers for different children, and I don't always get it right. But that's okay. Children don't need or expect perfection. Perfection doesn't build trust; open communication and a willingness to hang in there does. And I'm usually comfortable with my mistakes.

I know that if I want to focus on family life in my curriculum, I'm not going to get far without involving parents, and sometimes that creates conflict. But you can't get around it if you want to be effective, if you want to have a real impact on children's lives.

For me, it's scarier to make mistakes when I'm working with parents. I know that if I want to focus on family life in my curriculum, I'm not going to get far without involving parents, and sometimes that creates conflict. But you can't get around it if you want to be effective, if you want to have a real impact on children's lives. You have to learn how to listen and negotiate with parents. That's another challenge for me now.

Most of the ways we've involved parents in the past have been in support roles—fixing equipment, raising money, bringing in something to share. And we've always done parent education—parent meetings and classes, potlucks, handbooks and newsletters. Those are all good ways for parents to connect with the school, and some people get very involved, but I've been feeling something is missing. We're not getting parents involved in planning their child's education, and we're not getting our anti-bias ideas across.

But why should they listen to us? A few parents choose our school for the philosophy, but most choose us because we're convenient, or they've heard we're a good place, or because we're the campus child care center. They're busy, under pressure, and our ideas must seem irrelevant to their lives. I've spent a lot of time trying to "educate" parents, but now I have to ask, "How much time have I spent finding out what they want their child to learn?" I guess that should be obvious—find out what parents want for their children. To do that, I have to start lots of two-way discussions, and I have to develop trust. I have to focus on parents' issues, not mine, and model what I mean by respect.

When I have asked parents what they want, they usually talk about academic and social skills. I can find out what they do at home and what they expect me to do at school, and I can talk about how I teach those skills. That gets us off to a good start. But I've also learned that many people want to talk about what they don't want—they don't want their child to get dirty, or take off his or her shoes, or go to the bathroom with other children. Now I'm more willing to try out exceptions to our classroom routines. We've always done this with family food preferences, so I'm trying to include other family preferences, as well. I've been saying to particular children, "Your family wants you to stay dry" or "We'll set up screens for you in the bathroom" or "I'll help you keep your shoes on like your dad asked you to."

These special requests can drive me crazy when I get too many of them. And then I have to figure out how flexible I can be and still provide the structure children need to form a solid group. It's a tricky balance, and it varies from group to group. I have to know what my bottom lines are and what my school stands for, and I have to accept that not all families are going to agree.

My conflicts with parents rarely come to the extreme of a family leaving the center, because we can often find common ground. For instance, if a parent comes in and says, "If my child swears, just smack him on the face" (which has happened), I don't just refuse the request. I try to find a place of agreement to start from. For example, I might say, "No. I'm not willing to do that. Let's talk about what you want and what I want. You want your child to be respectful and so do I. Let's start from there."

I'm finding that if I take a deep breath, if I don't panic and get rigid and start sounding like an early childhood textbook about developmentally appropriate curriculum, I learn a lot from these discussions and conflicts. If I give the message that "I know the truth and you don't," I'll come off as trying to establish dominance. I'm setting up a power struggle. These beginning dialogues are more about listening and building trust, creating a partnership. Sure, I know a lot about this age group, but parents know more about their own children and how they behave within the family and out in the wider world. I need their input. And most parents want mine, once they trust me.

If I only pay attention to a person's race or gender, I'll miss a lot about that person. And if I look at them only as an individual, without a history and a culture, I also lose something important.

Most parents have had lousy experiences with institutions and with people in power. After all, parenting doesn't get much support or respect, mostly lip service. And memories of school aren't always positive. My school is an institution within an even bigger institution—a community college. Plus, I'm a white man. Many parents give me the benefit of the doubt, but it doesn't surprise me anymore when someone starts out on the defensive, expecting me to do something racist or sexist. It doesn't help if I get all huffy about that. I have to accept that I am a white man, and I represent a powerful, mostly white institution, and that I can be clueless about other people's cultures and points of view. Some people have been able to tell me how hard it can be to walk in our door when they're not white, or when they're poor, or if all their experience with school has been lousy. I've realized that the burden of getting a trusting relationship going is on me.

If I can get a respectful dialogue going with a parent (sometimes I can't, and that's where it's helpful to have a coteacher), that parent is more likely to confront me when they think something's wrong, rather than just write me off. Then the conflict can lead to a better relationship where my ideas are more likely to be heard.

Discussions only get you so far, though. Adults need to see concrete results, just like children. They're not going to trust me if I'm not responsive to their daily issues: "How do I get my child to school without tantrums?" "Why is my child swearing?" "Why won't she eat?" "Is my child okay?" "Am I an okay parent?" And they have questions about how we work with children to get them to solve their own problems: "Why aren't you disciplining these children?" "Why aren't you giving them time-outs?" So it takes a good chunk of the year to help parents see what we're doing, that our philosophy and process work for most of the children. Then we can get across our ideas about anti-bias curriculum. And some of those same parents who have a hard time become our biggest supporters.

Sometimes, by working through these conflicts, I get to hear how a person views the world from a different place. I learn something about their culture and family, and I hope they get to see how I view the world. We find out what we have in common, as well as our differences, and then we can really create a partnership to educate their child.

I think we live in a world where the different races, classes, and genders are taught to live in different cultures. I don't think that's necessary, but it's the reality. If I only pay attention to a person's race or gender, I'll miss a lot about that person. And if I look at them only as an individual, without a history and a culture, I also lose something important. I believe that even while you pay attention to a person's race, gender, ethnicity, and so on, you can see that person as a human being, just like everyone else in the world, and you can see that person as an individual, unlike anyone else in the world. People's lives have so many layers, so many currents flowing together. Sometimes the layers are in harmony, and sometimes they contradict one another. You can't really know someone without looking at all the layers at once. That's hard, because we're so complex, but if you ignore or pretend not to see part of a person, you are hurting them.

I believe people can learn to fully respect one another's lives, with all their layers and contradictions. And that's what I want to learn to do. That's the positive vision I try to keep in mind when I'm having a conflict with a parent. Of course, sometimes my vision is more about sticking my fingers in my ears and running away or sticking out my tongue and kicking them in the shin, but then I have my own layers to learn about too.

Once I start thinking about parents' lives, I'm forced to look at my own, to accept my own strengths and weaknesses, my own biases, my own history, to discover my own culture. As a white American, my life just seemed "normal," until I allowed myself to compare it to something different, with respect for the differences. Now it's like I'm six years old again, discovering that the whole world isn't Jewish. I'm discovering the many ways I'm American, white, male, Jewish, straight, a member of the Hoffman family—all by learning how other people think about food, clothing, education, a million issues, big and small.

And I'm reminded that this work is really about finding and challenging my own assumptions on gender, culture, disability, sexual orientation, and class. It helps to reflect on how my life has shaped me. How did I learn my assumptions? How do I pass them on to children? Which assumptions about right and wrong do I want to hold on to and pass on to children? Which are just biased judgments of other people's lives?

As a white, straight, American male, I know that women, people of color, and gays and lesbians have a lot of legitimate reasons not to trust me, to be afraid of me. But it doesn't help to travel with a load of paralyzing guilt. I would rather learn to be an activist, to find out how I can be effective. I know I'm not good at organizing a lot of people. I'm not that kind of a leader. But I am skilled at helping children with diversity issues, and I want to be able to help other adults learn those same skills, at my work and in my community. People often want a recipe for what to try next, what's doable, and that's difficult. They also need a positive vision they can work toward. I want to be able to help people with the details and inspire them as well.

I'm just starting to work in the larger community as part of a team of six teachers, counselors, parents, and diversity consultants to create a course for parents and child care workers on conflict resolution and diversity. It's been an exciting process and a lot of work to work so cooperatively, to understand a subject from different perspectives, and to help others see mine. In the past, most of my work experience has been with early childhood people who share my view and language, and I've learned that when I'm faced with a diversity of viewpoints, I tend to try solving problems alone. But for this project, the CRADLE project, we each do our own thinking, bring it to the group, and then create a consensus on what we want included. What a revelation! People have so many wonderful ideas to share and different perspectives to contribute! And some have the same ideas as I do, but they use different words to describe them.

Now when I hit a frustrating roadblock, I can tell myself, "Hey, with the great people I work with at Cabrillo and in the

CRADLE Project, I know that if I do my best, someone will pick up the other pieces, and we'll get this done. It's not my job to do it all."

So I've learned to value the process. I used to think that if I worked hard enough, I could come up with the "right answers" that would cure children of bias and make everybody happy. I don't believe that anymore. The solution to racism, sexism, and homophobia is to stop teaching children all that misinformation in the first place. I don't have the power to make that happen now, and anything I do once children are already infected by those lies is less than perfect. Anything I try will be unsatisfactory to someone, make someone uncomfortable, or cause a conflict. But if I try to meet every possible criticism before I take action, I will be paralyzed. So I've got to keep moving ahead with my best thinking, learn from the results, listen to the criticism, and try again.

If I try to meet every possible criticism before I take action, I will be paralyzed. So I've got to keep moving ahead with my best thinking, learn from the results, listen to the criticism, and try again.

I look at some of the things I've done in the past—activities that I now see as "tourist curriculum," things I've said to parents— and some seem naive and downright embarrassing. But I don't regret having done them—I wouldn't have come up with my current ideas if I hadn't tried those things that failed. Next week, or ten years from now, I'll read this essay and perhaps be embarrassed by some of my ideas. But it doesn't help to deny the past. It's what got me here. In two hundred years, when people read about the ways we treat children, the ways our culture handles diversity, I hope they'll be appalled, the same way I felt when I found out that the founding fathers of the United States kept slaves.

There have been so many times when I felt like I started out in one place, traveled a million miles, and then found that—Surprise!—the universe had put me right back at the beginning. That's okay, because now I'm getting over the feeling that there are thirty billion things that need to get done and I'm still stuck, all alone, on the first one. Now I know that this work is a journey. And now I know that I'm traveling with friends and a suitcase full of hope.

Discussion Questions

1. Eric writes about the changes he has made in his attitudes and interactions with parents. Can you imagine a situation when you'd feel justified in imposing your beliefs on families with whom you work? Why or why not? How much does it make sense to let one's professional practice as a teacher be changed by what parents want for their children? How do you decide where that line is?

2. Eric talks about using ordinary everyday activities to convey an anti-bias perspective. How might you change one activity that you do with children to align it with an anti-bias approach? How might you change one small routine in your personal life to more effectively align it with an anti-bias perspective?

3. Eric discusses some of the differences he grapples with as a man in a female-dominated field. What other gender-related issues do you think men who work in child care and early childhood education face? Do male parents face any similar gender-related issues in dealing with their children's early childhood care and education settings? Are there ways in which you think child care and early childhood education institutions could change to be more welcoming of men as teachers and parents?

June Labyzon

Finding Peace

I grew up in Union City, New Jersey, just three minutes through the Lincoln Tunnel from New York City. My family is Italian. When I was growing up in the fifties, my family was powerful in Union City. They just ran the city; the chief of police and the superintendent of schools were both from my family. And they also ran the gambling. So I grew up with an interesting background. The gambling aspect of my family's business was an important part of my life. It made me a gambler for the rest of my life, so I've always been willing to take chances.

Union City is where minorities settle after they've arrived in New York and find it too costly. Then, as they begin to "better" themselves, group by group they flee Union City for the suburbs, and another group moves in. When I was growing up, the newest minority groups were the Italians and the Irish. In the late fifties, the Cubans and Puerto Ricans came. Now Indonesian people are moving into Union City.

Yet in this city so rich with diversity, people don't share. Each little group has always kept to itself, so there's lots of misunderstanding and bigotry. I don't think I was aware of it when I was little. Everybody I was friends with and everybody in our neighborhood was Italian Catholic. There was also a large percentage of Jewish people in the city, but they didn't live on my block. I clearly remember our little houses located on one side of a big mirror factory. On the other side were the tenements where all the Irish people and the other "Americans" lived. My family always made a clear distinction between the "Italians" and the "Americans," at least while I was growing up. Those of us who lived on the "better" side of the mirror factory were not allowed to associate with the kids on the other side, and we didn't. We just didn't.

And we didn't like it when they came to our side. Sometimes the children would come and scare us, calling us names and threatening to beat us up. Occasionally they would vandalize our property. It wasn't until I was much older that I realized I spent a childhood picking up all sorts of messages. I never realized that my neighbors were crying out to be treated humanely. I didn't realize it until I started getting involved in doing anti-bias work and saw that there was plenty of bigotry within the white race.

It wasn't until I was much older that I realized I spent a childhood picking up all sorts of messages. I never realized that my neighbors were crying out to be treated humanely.

My mother, who's eighty now, was a teacher and librarian. At that time, it was unusual for a woman to have graduated from college, especially a prestigious one like New York University. Because she was a teacher, there was never any question what I would be. From the time I was really little, I was told that my brother was going to be a doctor and I was going to be a teacher. He became a veterinarian and I went to college to become a teacher. After my first year, I absolutely rebelled. I quit. I decided that I wasn't going to be a teacher just because my mother wanted me to be one.

I worked in New York City for five years, starting as a clerk-typist in an advertising agency and working my way up to administrative assistant. When I went back to school, I was determined that I wasn't going to become a teacher unless it was my own decision. I went to school at night for ten years. When I finally became certified to teach, it was because I knew

I wanted to work with young children. It made sense to me. I realized then what I still believe now—early childhood is an age when children's minds are very active, a time when you can really help them develop their talents. I knew that I could do that.

In 1968, when I was twenty-two, I married a man who was very active in underground politics and the whole flower child/hippie movement. That's when I began to change. No more isolated little Catholic Italian girl. Then, in 1972, we sold all our belongings and for four months lived in a Volkswagen van traveling cross-country to California and back. Life was never the same after that. I met many people who were doing some real things with their lives, and I wanted to be one of them.

In December of 1973 I received my teacher's certification. My husband wanted to leave Jersey, so I applied for jobs all over the country. One day I received a phone call from a school district in New Orleans. They asked only two questions: Are you white? and Are you willing to work in an all-black school? I said yes to both, and they told me I was hired.

Wait a minute, I wanted to scream! You don't know anything about me. Don't you even want to meet me? Don't you want to interview me? They said it wasn't really necessary. I explained that it was necessary to me. So I went down, walked into the school board office, and two women asked me some very insubstantial questions, which I answered. They told me I still had the job if I wanted it. Because I wasn't sure if I wanted to make such a big move, I said I'd let them know.

When I walked out of the building, I was suddenly surrounded by hundreds of angry African American faces. They were protesting something that had happened in one of the high schools—a student had died and they said it was the result of a beating from a white coach. I remember it vividly. I was in the middle of that crowd of people and I was wearing those high platform shoes that we used to wear in those days, when one of the heels just cracked off. I tried to pretend that I could walk normally, but several children noticed and started pointing at me and laughing. I just kept going, walking on my toes. I was mortified. That was my introduction to my new home, and I didn't know what to do.

I ended up in a school that gave me one of the most wonderful experiences of my life. Located on the outskirts of one of the housing projects, it was considered, at that time, a little college run by these old-time African American educators. It was a real tight ship, and the teachers were exceptional. Almost everything I've learned about functioning in this system and becoming the good teacher I am today is because of those teachers.

There were five white teachers in the school already, and they stuck together. Then there was me—skinny, dressed in long skirts with scarves tied on my head. The African American teachers took me under their wings and taught me so much during that difficult time. The second month I was there, my husband and I started having problems and split up. Plus, the class I had been given was made up of all of the children nobody else wanted. They were kindergarten kids, but they were already tough and disturbed.

I felt the children needed contact, so I did a lot of touching, a lot of singing. And I did a lot of visual arts. At that point in my life, I was not aware of how necessary it was to bring the children's cultures into the classroom. But I did bring myself into the classroom—totally. The only criticism I got was that I had "thousands" of art projects hanging from the ceiling and on the walls. (This school wasn't really into the arts.) But the other teachers saw that I was genuinely concerned about the kids, so they went along with me, and my principal acknowledged how hard I worked. It was still so terribly difficult.

At one point, feeling desperate, I went to the principal to tell her that I didn't think I was going to make it. She told me

that I had the right stuff and that I was going to be okay. But I've never been a person who was afraid to admit that I couldn't do something and I really wanted her to know that I was having a terrible time. In fact, I needed her to know that I was terrified. So she told me that she was going to get me some help...and she did.

Our school hosted the Community Opportunity Program, where mostly African American Vietnam vets who were going to night school at a local university could work as paraprofessionals in the classroom. In the mornings, they would work on reading with at-risk first and second graders. My principal asked one of the participants to help in my room in the afternoon. To make a long story short, she didn't know the kind of help she was giving me. He really did help me through. Several years later we wound up getting married and had a child.

*A*fter three years I changed schools, and it was at that time that I got involved, totally by accident, with three other teachers—an accident that changed my life. Together we got involved in Montessori education. Using grant money, we bought some Montessori materials and became certified in that way of teaching, earning master's degrees along the way. Our goal was to start a Montessori program for kindergarten and first grade in the projects, because we knew it would work well there. Finally, after a lot of trying, we were given a pilot program in two sister schools in the same housing project. Later, two of the teachers convinced an administrator to provide an empty building that could be used for a school. The first year there were just two classes. The second year there were four. Then the school moved again to the building it is in now.

In the beginning, there were six of us (four teachers, a principal, and a secretary) and 120 children. Now, our Montessori school, a magnet school, has become one of the number one schools in New Orleans. We have more than 700 children, and the school goes from kindergarten to eighth grade. Our families are varied—some very wealthy, some very poor. Our faculty and staff number is close to 60. Within our school we also have one of three French American schools in the United States which is certified by the French government. We have a good gifted resource program, a good arts connection dance program, and several resource programs for theater and the visual arts. We have an active parent body with a strong interest in their children's education. We are really a viable school, and I'm very proud of that.

With every joy comes sorrow. Though the school is a wonderful achievement, we weren't able to keep it in the housing projects. Also, one year while I was on leave, the proposal for the school was rewritten to keep a 50-50 diversity balance between African Americans and European Americans. That bothers me because I feel the population of the school should reflect the population of the city, which isn't 50-50, but closer to 70 percent African American. But I do understand the good intentions behind the idea of a 50-50 balance. And actually, in the past couple of years, I would say that we're 60 percent African American and 40 percent white and other people of color, which is a little closer to fair. A group of my colleagues are working on a new admissions policy, and we are all very excited about it.

And there are so many things that need working out. For instance, we don't have very many African American teachers—maybe four out of thirty, although the cafeteria and the custodial staff, of course, are all African American. That frustrates me and some of the other teachers. And though we've been pushing to get African American teachers, it just hasn't happened. Some of the African American parents are upset by this, though they acknowledge the excellent quality of our teachers and are pleased with them in general. They would like the school to have more role models of color for their children, which is completely understandable.

And there is institutional racism at our school, just as there is in all institutions of a racist society. It's not any worse at our school than anywhere else in New Orleans (in fact, I hope it's better), but you can't pretend that it doesn't exist. A few years ago, several staff members told me that if I would just keep my mouth shut, there would be no racism at our school. And they really believed that. It's easy to say, "We're not racist. Look at the population of our school. Look how wonderfully the kids get along." To be fair, I don't think people are consciously being racist when they say things like that. But then again, that's how most racism works. It doesn't have to be overt. Some of the teachers feel that the black parents use racism as a copout whenever their children don't do well or whenever they're unhappy about something. To be honest, maybe that happens some of the time, but I refuse to believe that it's often the case. I've tried to help people understand that if somebody feels that something racist is happening, if somebody hurts or feels they're being treated unfairly, it's real to them. You can't demean what someone says by screaming, "How dare you accuse me of being a racist?" You have to sit down together and talk about it, ask questions of each other. "What is it that is making you feel this way? Explain to me. Maybe I am doing something that is unkind. Maybe I am doing something unconsciously that is making you feel that I am acting in a racist way." That's the way to deal with it. But people get very angry and tell me they won't handle it that way because that would mean they're admitting to being racist. And to be fair, I used to react the same way.

As I think about our school, the teachers and the families, I can't help but reflect on who we all are and how we're involved in this work. I believe what people do stems from their personal interests and history. I know that when I had my child I began to look at life very, very differently. Still, for me, anti-bias work began way before then. I think it really started, without my realizing it, when I was about thirteen years old. My uncle had said something about the "niggers" that he worked with and I screamed at him—yelled and carried on. I told him that he was prejudiced and a bigot. I was being rude, but I had to tell him how I felt and what I thought.

At the same time, I can't say that I have never acted in a racist way. Reflection is part of anti-bias work, and honesty has to be a part of that reflection. So many of us have memories of racism that we've buried out of shame. In trying to understand myself and examining my memories, I have had to acknowledge parts of my life that I didn't want to remember at all. For example, when I was in my teens there was a woman in my father's family with whom I was infatuated. Her name was Snookie and I thought there was something about her that was just so special. She lived in Providence, and she would come to visit us several times a year. I remember her saying that she didn't want to eat at Chock Full-O-Nuts because she would be served by black people there, and she didn't like eating at Horn & Hardart's because she would have to eat with them. And so for a while, I made the same exact statements. She was my idol and I wanted to be like her. I know that happens to many teenagers, but it's hard to remember that I could have allowed myself to say such overtly racist things.

> *Reflection is part of anti-bias work, and honesty has to be a part of that reflection.*

My work really began in the early seventies, with all the protest marches in Washington and learning to be very open to all different kinds of people. And since, it has been evolving along with my life. My second husband was African American, and being with him flung me into an Afrocentric lifestyle. We separated in 1986, and it didn't take long to realize that I wasn't capable of raising an African American child by myself. I came to depend on a lot of my African American colleagues and friends and my husband's family to give my daughter the support that she needs. And as she's grown, there have been so many ways my daughter has influenced how I see my life and my work.

One really significant incident happened at about the same time. I was on a committee to get more black teachers on our faculty. Fifty percent of our students were African American, yet we had only one African American teacher, and all the rest were white. At a meeting, one of the African American parents made a remark that I told him was a dangerous thing to say. I thought that he knew I was his ally, but he stood up with his fist in the air. Slamming it on the table, he pointed his finger in my face and said, "You are the dangerous one. I've watched you for this entire year, and what you do around here is perpetuate the racism." He went on and on, and I was devastated. My daughter and all the parents were sitting there, of course. Everybody started coming to me and putting their hands on my shoulders. But I was angry, mainly because he had said that to me in front of my child.

A few days later, I saw him at a public function—a celebration of the African American child. He came up to me, hugged me, and said to my daughter, "Your mother's mad at me right now. But she and I are a lot alike. We're both freedom riders. We just do it in a different way."

I kept thinking about what he had said. Every time I saw him he would be friendly. After a long time, I realized that he was telling me to keep fighting. He didn't say what he did to anybody else there. He chose to say it to me because he knew that I consciously wanted to work to make things better. He knew that it would spur something in me. And I also realized that what he had said was true. I wasn't consciously being racist, but I was allowing those around me to get away with being racist. At the meeting, I had come to the defense of someone who had made a very racist statement. And that was what he meant. To this day, I credit this man for the work that I do because he knew what he was doing, and he was betting on the result.

It was around that same time that a friend called me to say, "Look, June. I've got something you really need to do, but you need to do it by Monday." Then she gave me Louise Derman-Sparks' book *Anti-Bias Curriculum* and some information about the Culturally Relevant Anti-Bias (CRAB)

Leadership Project, and I sat down and read all of it. She was right. This was something I really wanted to do. So I wrote out my application to be involved with the project for three years, and my life has not been the same since.

Our group started out with about eighteen people, dwindling later to thirteen. We met monthly and also had retreats. And we worked on developing an anti-bias curriculum.

I was the only teacher in the group. The others were early childhood advocates and some anti-racist community activists, working with adults doing early childhood workshops and seminars. I took what I learned from the group, brought it to my school, and ran an anti-bias curriculum in my classroom to the best of my ability.

It was a tremendous three years with that group—taking me from zero on a scale of ten to maybe a five or six, which was tremendous growth for me. I think that in this line of work you have to keep growing. I don't think I'll ever reach point ten before I die, though I can't help but hope.

The first time our group got together, we met for a whole week. We went through the *Anti-Bias Curriculum* book. We went through issues. We divided into racial groups (we had an even number of white and black women) and hashed out our problems among one other. We came back together and went even deeper. We had upheavals, and it seemed like every time I left a meeting I said that I was never going back. It was just so painful—facing yourself, facing issues, seeing sides of yourself that you didn't want to see, thinking you were one way and finding you were another. I wasn't the only one who had a hard time. Many times people would say they were not going to come back, and some would drop out for a while and return later. But the first week we got together— that was a really wonderful week.

> *I have come to realize that guilt is the crutch we use to keep ourselves from growing.*

The hardest thing for me was that I had never seen myself as white. I had always seen myself as Italian, and I had separated that from being white. But two of the white women in the group would not let me get away with it. They helped me to understand what they were talking about, that whatever my cultural identity, I had a position of privilege within the system of racism because of my white skin. I came to understand that in addition to my cultural identity (Italian), I have a racial identity put on me by institutional racism, which is white.

Immediately following that week I went to the People's Institute for Survival and Beyond, an anti-racist training organization in New Orleans, and attended a training called "Undoing Racism." It really helped me understand how to organize and made the institutional racism piece clearer for me. At that point, I began to say, "Yes, all white people are racist. I am racist. But I'm working actively to be anti-racist." Since then I've attended the same training two more times, and now they've expanded the cultural piece.

The training changed me a lot. I truly believe that all white people are racist because of the racist system of white privilege in which we all live, and that we have to work at living with an anti-racist perspective. Now when I see things in myself that I know aren't right, rather than trying to push them away, I pull them out, look at them, and ask myself, "What are you saying here?" And I work at finding perspective. Before, when I did something that I felt was bigoted or racist, I wouldn't do anything about it; I would just feel guilty. I have come to realize that guilt is the crutch we use to keep ourselves from growing. I just recently turned fifty, and my new slogan in life is, "Just get over it." Push beyond the guilt, because it's too easy to take comfort in it.

I know that I carry stereotypes. For example, I noticed that seeing a black man walking down the street made me pull my purse closer. I had to ask myself what that was about. Was it maybe because I was mugged? After asking myself questions and paying attention to my own behavior for a while, now I'm clear that I pull my purse closer when any person is approaching me on the street. But I had to pay attention to my own behavior to find that out. I've also been able to work on the stereotypes that we have in society—the stereotypes that I've taken in—that certain races are either good or bad at certain things. Some people may want to say that those kinds of statements are the truth, but I say they're racist. And these issues are acute because I'm trying to raise an African American female by myself. So I have to be doubly sure that I'm not employing racism in my own home, against my own child.

Anti-bias work is about the way you treat people, the way you treat children. So at school, even when I thought that I wasn't meeting the kids' needs by bringing their different cultures into my room, I was. It wasn't to the extent that I am now doing it, but I was doing whatever I could to adjust to their different learning styles. In my classroom, if a child needed to work on art, he or she worked on art. One little boy could only learn by following me around, so he did. I believe he actually learned through assimilation.

At my school now, I have a special opportunity because I work with the same children for two years, sometimes three, so we are able to have a family grouping—four year olds to eight year olds—children at different levels of development working with one another. Actually, there are usually twenty-five kids on twenty-five different levels, and I am able to get to know them as people. As part of the Montessori curriculum, we observe rather than teach. So I spend a lot of time looking, touching, and talking to my kids. And if I have a special gift, it's that I can really tune in.

I realize that I have faults to overcome. I know that I tend to yell when I get excited, and sometimes I yell at the kids. I like to say it's because I'm a New York Italian, but it's a part of me that I'm trying to curb because I know that no one likes to be yelled at. At the same time, I always say to the kids that after they've been a part of my classroom and learned to deal with me, they can function anywhere and with anyone. And they understand because they like me.

I have a "just do it" approach, and that has sometimes been a hindrance. I went overboard when I was just beginning my work, which was very damaging. My classroom was about

60 percent African American. Two children were from India, one from Japan, one from Nicaragua, and the rest of the children were white. I went in, I'm still not sure why, and made my curriculum totally Afrocentric. I know that I felt that I hadn't been doing enough for the African American kids, and they were in the majority. The white kids didn't react negatively, but the little girl from Nicaragua started acting out—hurting people, coming into the building at lunchtime and stealing things from the computer room. Her behavior was just awful. She wasn't paying attention during group lessons. She wasn't doing anything. Then one day I happened to pick up a couple of books in a bookstore. One was on learning about your Hispanic American culture. I brought that book and several others into the classroom and put them out. I told her that one of the books was just for her. Within two days, she was totally different.

That helped me to realize that I had made the classroom a totally unacceptable place for her. It wasn't safe. I needed to do more with her culture. Now I write a letter to parents every year saying that I value family culture in my classroom and explain what that means. Then I ask that they come in and give a presentation with their child about what is really significant to their family culture. I emphasize that this does not just mean their ethnic culture, but the things that they do as a family, who they are, and where they're from. This was very successful with the parents from India. They brought in videos of their country and explained how they were married through matchmaking, which was very unusual for the kids to hear. We even re-created the whole wedding ceremony. Some parents have brought things in for the kids to taste. A Japanese family would send in a little history each time their child brought in snacks. It was very difficult to get the parents of the little girl from Nicaragua to come in, but when her mother finally did, it was an insight for me. I found out how shy and young she

Anti-bias work is about the way you treat people, the way you treat children.

was. I'm glad I remedied my approach in the classroom. It sensitized me from then on.

As I continued to encourage families to share their cultures, I became the teacher that many of the Jehovah's Witnesses requested. Many people are very judgmental and cruel when it comes to religion. It seems to me that some teachers who are lenient with racial issues have trouble with religious ones. I have a lot of Jehovah's Witnesses in my class every year, and when we do family culture and sharing, they bring in their films and literature to share with the children and other families. We look at their ways as part of real-life culture, not religious indoctrination. And when we celebrate the few holidays that we do, there are options for children who don't celebrate. We don't make it a big deal. Over the years, families that have lots of differences request me.

Also, from the very beginning of school, I try to use as many culturally relevant materials and information as possible. I keep the material out all year rather than put things away as we finish discussing a particular area of the world. I don't want the kids to think that they move in and out of importance. I want them to see themselves in the classroom all of the time and never think their position in the classroom isn't stable.

When kids are treated with this kind of sensitivity, they do get it. One of my favorite anecdotes is about a little boy who I had in class for two years. One day he looked up at me out of the blue and said, "Miss June, I finally understand. Culture is all those things that we do with our family. All of those things that we are. And race is just the way people look at us because of the color of our skin." He said it in simple language, and though it took him two years, he understood—he wasn't his race, he was his culture. And that was his being.

Recently we had an exciting time in terms of curriculum. Alice, a very outspoken African American teacher from St. Louis, joined our school. She inspired another African American teacher on staff, and the three of us worked together as friends and colleagues. The first year Alice was with us, we had many African American celebrations, and it was wonderful. Each grade put on a presentation, and Alice and I coordinated with a parent in our school who's a very well-known musician. In our presentation, we talked about the Montgomery bus riots and other things like that—we sang the songs—and the children in my classroom, in essence, taught a lesson to the rest of the school.

But not everyone felt positively about it. Some of the parents thought we were dealing too heavily in African American curriculum. And some of the reactions I saw and felt among our staff disturbed me greatly. So I decided to bring it up in our anti-bias group. One of the other white women in the group told me about something that happened to her. She had been working with a group of predominantly white teachers to help their school do more with African American culture. She brought an African American woman to the staff meeting to lead a discussion, encourage dialogue, and offer ideas. After the meeting, one of the women on the staff who she thought of as a friend and ally approached her angrily, saying that the meeting had been a waste of her time and it was her fault. She stormed out of the meeting and to her car so there was no time to talk. My anti-bias colleague tried to initiate a discussion with her in a number of ways, but the person avoided any confrontation. When she finally had a chance to speak to the woman, she said, "Half of the children in your class are African American. You owe it to them to investigate your feelings." The teacher replied that she had no time to talk, and there wasn't really any need to because there just wasn't a problem. When pressed, she said, "You're supposed to be my friend. If you were, you wouldn't have started all this and right now you'd be taking my side instead of the person you brought to our school." My anti-bias colleague took a deep breath and explained that she wasn't taking a personal side. She was taking the side she believed in. She said, "This isn't about friendship. What you're really telling me is that I am white and because I am white I'm supposed to side with you and not take the side of someone who is black."

This was so much like an incident at my school involving a colleague and myself that I was astounded. Recently I had a confrontation with a friend I work with. We had not been doing well for a very long time, and one of the things I've been trying to do since I've become fifty is clean my slate, so I asked her to go to breakfast. She got very intense and told me, "June, this is all your fault. You got involved in all this anti-bias, undoing racism kind of stuff and you want to say that we're all racist. You think your anti-bias stuff is the right way, and as long as you continue, we won't be able to be friends."

I asked my anti-bias colleague what happened in the end with her situation, and she sighed. She had told the woman to think about what she'd said and now could only hope that she had. I knew how she felt, and I could also feel her weariness.

This work is hard. So hard that last year I knew I needed a sabbatical. I had a student teacher from Vietnam who didn't want to identify as being Vietnamese. Insensitively, I had pushed her to share her culture. She saw me as racist, and I was. I was steering her to do something she didn't want to do. I kept making too much of it. When I recognized what I was doing, after twenty-one years of teaching, I gave up. I just had to take a break. I didn't work the last four months of the school year, and then I took a year off.

This work gives me joy. Nurturing children in the classroom, putting out materials they can relate to—that gives me joy. Seeing them talking to one another about issues or ideas. Hearing them discuss ideas that I've presented. Watching them reach understandings of what I'm trying to explain. All of this gives me joy.

I thought my sabbatical would be a break, a time when I could allow myself not to grow. Instead, I allowed myself to rest, and from that rest, I have grown in ways I couldn't have predicted. At the beginning I didn't know what to do. I had always been at school, and so I had a hard time separating. But I lived my life the same way during that time off, from an anti-racist perspective. I just didn't do any work. I didn't go to any of the meetings. I just worked with my child and took a break. When I was near the end, I found myself telling everybody that I wished it was just the beginning because now I knew how to use the time. Many things have come out of it. I started involving myself in the theater community. Because that community here is so racially divided, what I want to do now is find how I can do anti-bias work with them.

When I went back to teaching, I was ready to begin again. I felt reborn. Now I want to do everything in my room through theater, storytelling, and creative writing. I don't know how successful it's going to be, but that's my goal, and I'm going to keep pushing myself toward it. I'm also going to try to be a little bit more mellow, maybe not as zealous. I intend to do things in a more subtle yet proactive way—intertwining everything through the arts. And I intend to teach the children to be proactive, as well. I want to give them accurate information about bias and teach them how to use it.

I knew that coming back would be hard because I'm in a very lonely position. While I was on sabbatical, the other teacher who was doing anti-bias work moved back home, so with both of us gone, I think the staff breathed a big sigh of relief and returned to their old ways. But the kindergarten teachers are beginning to come together, and this gives me hope. The Montessori curriculum helps too, because it's so conducive to an anti-bias curriculum. This work gives me joy. Nurturing children in the classroom, putting out materials they can relate to—that gives me joy. Seeing them talking to one another about issues or ideas. Hearing them discuss ideas that I've presented. Watching them reach understandings of what I'm trying to explain. All of this gives me joy. There is so much joy for me in seeing children being comfortable in the classroom and with me, seeing children be happy.

Now I am asking how I can get the strength to continue to do what I need to do. Support is so important. The anti-bias group was good, but most of the people were community organizers, not teachers. I get support from two of the white women in my anti-bias group who have since become my close friends (and, incidentally, now allow me to say I'm Italian). They're both also involved with the People's Institute. I also get support from an African American couple—a husband and wife—both of whom are my best friends in different ways. They've helped me support my daughter and my ideas. But I'd also like a national support system for those of us in situations like mine—those of us who are the only people in our schools trying to do this kind of work. I know I'm not the only one who's alone. So if you are someone starting out in this work, I offer these words of caution—get a suit of armor, and even more important, know yourself well. Be strong in your convictions. Don't do this work because you think it's the right thing to do or because you want to look good to other people or be liked. Do it because you have to, because this work is your way of life. Realize that once you begin, this work is a lifetime commitment.

Each year I make incredible mistakes—mistakes that make me want to put my head in the ground. And I'm still ashamed of some of the things that happened my first three years. At the same time, I've learned so much. And even though there's so much more growing to do, I know that now my entire life and my approach to life is different.

Most of all, I hope that I'll never stop growing. None of us is perfect, but we are the kind of people who strive for perfectionism. I don't ever envision myself, even before I die, being 50 percent of where I'd like to be. There's just so much to do. It's a long journey with enormous goals. At this point in my life, however, I just want to achieve a sense of peace within myself and a sense of peace in the people I deal with on a daily basis. And I think that the only way I can achieve peace will be to treat everybody as humanly as possible.

Discussion Questions

1. June cautions other anti-bias educators to "know yourself well." Why do you think she suggests this? What do you think you might need to know about yourself in order to do good anti-bias work? How do you think you might go about learning it?

2. June describes several tensions between herself and co-workers arising from her anti-bias perspective. Have you experienced similar conflicts? How have you responded? What has been most effective, in your experience?

3. June discusses tension with her own family because of their different views about racial equality and lack of support for her anti-bias work. This is not uncommon. Do you face similar family tensions? How have you resolved them?

Beth Wallace

Seeking Wholeness

A nti-bias work is so intertwined with my life and how I grew up that it would be impossible for me to isolate one moment or one factor and say, "There! That's where it all began." Pulling at any one strand brings the whole tangle with it.

I think of my father, who raised me to cleave to the truth, to stand up for whatever I believed in regardless of the consequences. And my mother, who taught me compassion, showed me the beauty in the natural world, and demonstrated the complexity of being human. I think of being ostracized in elementary school and physically threatened by other children, for reasons that I have yet to understand. Probably it had something to do with the class split in the small town I grew up in. Whatever the exact reason, that experience wakened in me a kind of fury against injustice that still moves me today. I think of the slow journey of my twenties, when I recognized my cultural identity as a rural New England Yankee; when I came out as a lesbian; when I started to learn about racism, classism, and other oppressions and to confront them in myself and others. Through all of my adult life I have worked with children, and I have never separated that work from my thinking about social justice. On the contrary, the two seem natural partners. What better way to change the world than to work with children? What better way is there to work with children than to examine the world we find around us and try to make sense of it together?

I grew up in rural Vermont in the sixties and seventies, with a strong sense of connection both to the land and to rural culture. I didn't grow up on a farm, but I did grow up surrounded by farms and farm kids. I am a sixth-generation Vermonter on my mother's side. I was raised to think of that as significant, to think of myself as rooted in the stony soil and the worn-down old mountains of Vermont. When it comes to social justice and anti-bias work, there are many ways that rural Yankee culture supports me. There are long-standing traditions of independence and equity in Vermont. There was a strong social justice movement there when I was growing up, and I became a part of it as I got older. There is a stated belief in treating people equitably and traditional forms of solving problems in community—town meeting day, for example, where everyone comes together to have open discussions and make decisions together.

What better way to change the world than to work with children? What better way is there to work with children than to examine the world we find around us and try to make sense of it together?

On the other hand, people in Vermont often don't have much experience with cultural differences. As Minnesota anti-bias educator Mary Loven has said about the rural areas of that state, there is such a strong message that racism is abhorrent that many white people are afraid of exploring issues about racism. They resist even thinking about it because the possibility of being perceived as racist is so loathsome. As a result, there's an undercurrent of bigotry that is sometimes harder to see or address because it's so hidden. I always think of a poem by Audre Lorde in which she describes driving through Vermont in the summer and how beautiful it is. Passing two teenage boys cutting hay, she sees one wave—and hears the other shout, "Nigger!" That contradictory image is compelling to me because it illuminates a truth about Vermont and

Yankee culture that has confounded me for much of my life. There really is a basic belief in equity and independence, a kind of openness to difference, and at the same time there are also the same institutional and personal forms of oppression that are the scourge of our country.

It probably took me longer to understand racism, for example, because of the way people around me in Vermont were thinking about it. When I was growing up, the adults in my life believed, and told me, that racism had ended with the civil rights movement. I was taught that it was possible for individuals to display bigoted behavior, and of course this was not okay. But the idea of institutional racism, even as a thing of the past, was never explored. Segregation was presented as something that happened down South but would never occur where we lived (with the strong implication that we were more enlightened). When people did talk about racism, it was the color-blind "people are all the same underneath" stuff, or telling the story of how Vermonters were part of helping slaves escape to Canada by way of the Underground Railroad.

They didn't talk about the KKK burning crosses early in the century on Lyme Emory, a hillside in the small Vermont town of Washington. It wasn't until I was an adult that I heard the story of one of my older Vermonter friends whose sister wouldn't agree to marry a man until he had joined the KKK with her. As a result, when I went out in the world as an adult, I felt that I'd been lied to and betrayed by the adults I had trusted to tell me the truth about things. I felt that I'd been brought up ignorant, not taught how to examine the messages I was getting from the society around me, not given accurate information or skills to deal with the divisions between me and people I wanted to interact with. My passion about anti-bias education stems in many ways from that experience.

My ignorance growing up was exacerbated by the fact that there were literally no people of color living in my hometown. In Montpelier, the state capital and the next town over, there were only two African American families. There are more people of color in Vermont now (though still less than 10 percent of the state's population), but as a child I didn't come in contact with anyone who might have caused me to question the prevailing views. Of course, if people had been paying attention or had been adequately informed, they would have seen racism everywhere. But no one in my life was paying attention or thought it was important. The message was that race wasn't an issue—and in my daily life, that was true.

Class was the big issue, and it still is the immediate one for most kids growing up in Vermont. As a child, I got a lot of subtle messages about being better than other people because they were poor or working class. I also got some very clear messages about the differences between Montpelier, which is predominately middle and upper middle class, and its twin city of Barre, which has more of a working-class history. And I was certainly indoctrinated with middle-class values and culture. At the same time, many of my friends were working class, and the differences I had to sort through in those relationships I now see as being primarily about class. I had friends who lived in public housing. I had friends whose dads were in jail. These situations were completely outside my experience and the experience of my family. The lives of my friends—the food they ate, where they lived, what they did for fun, what was expected of them in school and at home, what they expected of friendships, the language they used—were different from mine in ways that I was being brought up not to value. How was I to make sense of these differences? I was brought up, at least implicitly, to believe in the United States as a classless society where people achieved by hard work and merit, and yet it was clear to me that my friends' par-

> The lives of my friends—the food they ate, where they lived, what they did for fun, what was expected of them in school and at home, what they expected of friendships, the language they used—were different from mine in ways that I was being brought up not to value. How was I to make sense of these differences?

ents worked hard—so why were they poor? The confusion and uncertainty I struggled with as a child was about these kinds of class issues. I think work around oppression often *is* confusing. It's not straightforward. It is difficult to try to untangle our visceral experiences and everything we were taught implicitly and explicitly, and then understand how all of it jibes with what we know intellectually about institutionalized oppression. The challenge is to embrace that complexity and confusion and all those feelings and work through them to some kind of inner clarity.

*L*ike many of us, I was feeling my way toward anti-bias work long before I had ever heard the word. In college, I trained to teach French, but I became increasingly uncomfortable with public schools. I had a difficult time articulating my dissent—I just knew that most of the schools I'd been in were not good places for most of the kids, and they probably wouldn't be good places for me. It had something to do with *what* was taught and *how* it was taught, how much of the real stuff of children's lives was missing, and how inequities in power were perpetuated. At the same time, I was passionate about the *idea* of public schools and dismayed by the elitism I saw in private schools, where some of the teaching that interested me was taking place, but primarily with a select student body (mostly white, mostly upper middle class). Now I read *Rethinking Schools*, a quarterly journal that addresses these issues in the context of public schools, and I get very excited about what some public school teachers are doing. But fifteen years ago, I didn't even know that kind of teaching was possible or how to go about looking for it. Deep inside I think I felt that I would get ground up in the public schools, that I would end up doing work that was in opposition to my deep convictions. I knew I wasn't clear enough intellectually (in the sense

of having enough information) or strong enough emotionally to hold my own against the weight of that system.

And so, shortly after graduating from college, I ended up in child care, working in the morning with preschoolers, and in the afternoon with school-age children. Both programs had well-deserved excellent reputations in the community. I learned so much from the teachers there. The two women I worked most closely with, Fran Solin and Mary Foote, were life-affirming people and fabulous teachers. I still learn from them, whenever we come in contact. However, the issues that troubled me in public schools didn't vanish in these more child-centered settings. In each program I had experiences that led me to question the work we were doing and to reach for a deeper and more honest way of working with the children, what I would now define as an anti-bias approach.

For example, in the after-school program I noticed that every day when we offered an active game in the gym, such as end zone/free zone, dodgeball, ultimate frisbee, or even kick-ball, most of the kids who chose to play were boys, even though the program was divided about evenly between boys and girls. The boys were much more competent at these sports, as well— they knew the rules, they weren't afraid of getting hit by the ball, their movements were strong, fluid, and confi-dent—and they dominated the play even when a few girls came along. When I talked to the girls about why they didn't come to the gym, they said they wanted to but they didn't know how to play the games, they didn't feel comfort-able with the equipment, and the boys made fun of them or took over. Meanwhile, of course, the girls excelled at more quiet, artis-tic pursuits, and while the boys were off ram-paging around the gym, the girls made com-plex craft projects. I wasn't quite sure what to do, but I felt clear that there was a problem, so I proposed a girls' day in the gym, once a week, so the girls could learn to play the active games without feeling incompetent and being put down by the boys. Almost every girl in the program was interested in participating, but the idea was nixed by the program director, who felt that it wouldn't be fair to the boys—after all, the girls were free to go to the gym every day, and the fact that the boys dominated wasn't their fault, so why should they be punished for it? None of the other staff members felt that the gender imbalance in the gym was a problem. "What would we do with the boys, and all that energy, if they didn't go to the gym to run it off?" they asked. I wasn't sure I had the right solution, but I was convinced that simply accepting the status quo wasn't right either. I felt confused and frustrated by the reaction of the other staff members, and I didn't have a good answer for their ques-tions, so I dropped the issue.

In each program I had experiences that led me to question the work we were doing and to reach for a deeper and more honest way of working with the children, what I would now define as an anti-bias approach.

At the same time, in the morning preschool, we were working with a Deaf three year old. His IEP (Individual

Education Plan) focused on his wearing hearing aids (which he hated), learning to speak, and using English. At a staff meeting, I talked about how frustrated I was with that approach. Because I had been introduced to American Sign Language (ASL) and to Deaf culture, it seemed clear to me that he should be in a signing environment and learning ASL as his primary language. I thought we should be helping his parents (who were hearing) understand that, in order for him to develop language, he needed ASL and to be around other Deaf people. Instead of trying to make him function in the hearing world, I felt that it was our responsibility to start facilitating his entry into Deaf culture and language. In the staff meeting, when I was trying to explain all this and feeling inarticulate about why it was so important, all I could come up with was that it was not just a pedagogical issue, but a political one. One of the other individual tutors said to me, "Beth, he's three years old. He doesn't know anything about politics." I had no idea how to respond to her, but Fran, the teacher, said, "Beth is saying that this is a liberation issue."

I don't think anything changed with that particular child, but Fran's statement helped to crystallize my thinking. At that moment, I began to make a conscious connection between my sense that something was being overlooked in our work with children and my growing political understanding of the dynamics of oppression. I didn't know what to do with that information or how to begin acting out of it, but inside me the conviction began to grow that somehow there had to be a way to use my passion for social justice to inform my work with children.

And then I was hired as the lead preschool teacher and the director at a little parent co-op day care center in Worcester, Vermont. I was absolutely floored when they offered me the job, because I was stupendously underqualified—I had no administrative experience, no supervisory experience, and only three months of preschool teaching experience. I had only applied because one of the center's board members had encouraged me. But it was a little tiny center, the kind that is always hovering on the edge (if you lose one kid you can't pay your bills) and they were only offering six dollars an hour with essentially no benefits. They didn't have a lot of options, and in many ways, neither did I. We were a good match.

What a learning experience! The first year I learned how much I didn't know. For instance, I knew nothing about managing nonprofits and nothing about how to help the board be effective or even what they were supposed to be doing. I didn't know how to manage an organizational budget, do the accounting, or figure out if we were breaking even. I had no training in early childhood, and I really didn't know how to teach. I had never supervised anyone, and I was uncomfortable taking authority. It was definitely trial by fire. But the children, of course, were wonderful, the families were very involved in the life of the center, and the setting was terrific—the ground floor of an old schoolhouse off the main road in a village with a population of 800. There were fields and woods around the center, and ponds and brooks within exploring distance. It was very much like where I grew up in Northfield.

Among the twenty or so families at the center, there was real variation in class, but not much racial, ethnic, or cultural diversity. The kids were mostly European American. Over the course of the three years I spent there we had one African American and two Korean American children, all of whom had been adopted by European American families, and two bicultural Anglo-Latino children. Only about half the children were at the center full-time; the rest attended on part-time schedules, which varied from family to family. We had a maximum of fourteen children at a time, ranging in age from two to six. I taught thirty to thirty-five hours a week, and directed in the other five, supervising two or three other staff members, most of whom worked part-time for five dollars an hour. Looking back on it, it sounds so wacky to try to run a program that way, but that's how it still is for many small centers.

Many of the families were living in poverty. There were also families with middle-class backgrounds who didn't have a lot of money because of the choices they'd made about their lifestyles. Still others had money and access to many resources. Most of the families were culturally Christian, but we always had at least one Jewish family too. So the parents were pretty diverse and had very different expectations for their children and for the work we would do with them, even though they were almost all white.

I was so isolated as a director and in the early childhood profession. I hadn't even heard of NAEYC then, and I didn't subscribe to any of the early childhood periodicals. Even though I think this was about the time that the *Anti-Bias Curriculum* book came out, I still hadn't heard of anti-bias education. But it was obvious to me that the families at Worcester Child Care had huge differences in class and in parent expectations. I had read some books about multiculturalism, but they only talked about race and ethnicity. They didn't go far enough or deep enough, and they didn't seem to be about social justice. Now I would probably call them tourist curriculum, but then I just knew that they didn't feel right. For example, none of them could help me figure out what to do about celebrating Christmas, which was important to many families at the center but was exclusionary not only for the Jewish families but also for Jehovah's Witness families. And they certainly didn't help me understand or manage the conflicts that arose around curriculum that seemed to me to be tied in with class and culture. The rock I clung to during those early years was the need to honor each child and each family's truths about themselves, and somehow balance those differences respectfully.

For instance, one year the kids went through a period of playing cop games, chasing and putting one another in "jail."

> *The rock I clung to during those early years was the need to honor each child and each family's truths about themselves, and somehow balance those differences respectfully.*

This troubled some of the parents. One upper-middle-class parent in particular was upset because she had taught her children that police officers were their friends and that people put themselves in jail by their actions. Because this was what she wanted her children to believe, she was disturbed by the game and wanted me to stop it. At the same time, there was a child in the class whose dad had been taken to jail by the state police for driving with a suspended license. This family were neighbors of mine, and so I knew that the only time the dad drove was when he went a half-mile down a dirt road every day to feed his horses. He felt that he had been obeying the spirit of the suspension. He and his wife were convinced that the cops had a grudge against him and had pulled him over vindictively. In addition, their son had seen his father get pulled over and arrested. For him, the theme of cops taking people to jail was real and immediate. It would have been absurd for me to say to that child, "Police officers are your friends." Instead I could (and did) say, "Cops don't put little kids in jail," and talk about all the things police officers do besides putting people in jail. Still, that kid's reality was the cops coming and taking his dad away. It would have been wrong for me to deny that experience.

And, of course, the larger social reality is that police officers are not seen (and do not act) uniformly as friends and helpers and defenders of justice, even by children. To say that people put themselves in jail by their actions overlooks the role of institutional racism and classism in the justice and penal system. That view of the world is both class-based and race-based, and even in a tiny center in Vermont, it didn't ring true for all the children. So to teach children that police officers are their friends is to teach a white middle-class view of the world. It doesn't affirm the truths of the lives of all the children; it creates a split between school and home for kids who have other experiences. It also contributes to a kind of tunnel vision on the part of middle-class children who only see their experience reflected in the school and don't have to confront other experiences or the role of privilege in their lives. Finally, it doesn't encourage the sharing of diverse truths and the examining of that complexity, which is what the anti-bias approach is all about.

We also had conflicts at Worcester Child Care that I came to ascribe to a clash between urban and rural cultures. Probably the clearest example of this was the disagreement around gun play, which is such an issue for child care teachers everywhere. Like many teachers, I was (and am) very uncomfortable with gun play. I think kids see way too much violence on television and in movies, and too often experience violence in their own lives. I see how the violence in our culture is communicated to children, how they are drenched in it, and how it then comes out in their play. At the same time, as a rural person, I know that there is a very real difference in the urban view and the rural view of guns. In an urban setting, the only thing you can do with a gun is hurt somebody. In a rural setting, that's simply not true. Guns are also tools that people use to get food for their families. Who hunts, who doesn't hunt, and how people hunt often (though not always) falls along class and culture lines. Guns used as tools, similar to and as dangerous as chain saws, are part of many children's lives.

This issue about guns and hunting points out to me the necessity of understanding history and exploring cultural roots when thinking about anti-bias work. In Vermont, there is a long class history bound up in hunting, going all the way back to the early immigrants from the British Isles, a history that adds intensity to the debates around guns and hunting today. In those days, throughout Britain and Europe, common folk weren't allowed to hunt freely because the land and the game on it belonged to the nobility. As a result, many poor people starved, literally in the midst of plenty, or they were hung or deported for "poaching." When people immigrated to North America, being free to hunt to feed themselves was not something they took for granted. This history has been forgotten by most people, but it has come down in rural culture in New England in many ways, including a strong local tradition of free trespass. No matter who actually owns the land, it has traditionally been okay for anyone to hunt or fish or simply walk there.

Adding to the complexity of this issue, the history is repeated today by people from more urban areas outside Vermont, many of whom have more access to money and resources than most people who grew up in the area. They move to Vermont or buy a piece of land for a second home, and often they immediately post No Hunting, No Fishing, No Trespassing signs. It's understandable that they want privacy and to feel safe on "their" land. But this practice repeats class history: Once again, people with more money (many of whom don't even live on the land for most of the year) are denying access to the land to people with less money (many of whom have roamed those woods for most of their lives). It raises some deep questions about who the land really belongs to and who gets to decide how it's used. And I think that when these different groups argue about hunting, as in many other kinds of cross-cultural conversations, they're not even really discussing the same things.

So the whole issue of gun play at the center was fraught with mostly unspoken class and cultural tensions, as well as all of the standard issues about violence and children's play. Some of the families of the children in the center hunted. Some staff members' families hunted. Everyone for sure had neighbors who used hunting as a way of supplementing their families' grocery budgets. Some families felt very strongly that hunting was immoral. Some families didn't eat meat at all. Some families who came from more urban cultures were really afraid of guns and wanted us to tell children that guns were bad because they hurt people. For some families, gun safety was a big issue. It was all very complicated. But it was also clear to me that it wasn't okay for us to tell the children that guns were bad and wrong. It wasn't culturally relevant in rural Vermont—and again, it was denying the truths of the real lives of some children and families.

At the same time, we did have a policy against war toys, and it wasn't okay with me to have kids shooting at each other with sticks, their fingers, or whatever. So I would say, "Guns are tools that some grown-ups use. They're not tools that we ever use to hurt people." That didn't always satisfy parents who came from more urban areas where a gun was an object of fear and a tool of violence, but it was the closest I could come to honoring the center families' complex feelings and different truths about guns and hunting.

In my experience, the most powerful place to begin anti-bias work is with children's real experiences and conflicts with each other and with other people in their daily lives.

It seems clear to me that anti-bias education is important wherever you are. I also believe that like any good curriculum, it has to take different forms that are relevant to each setting. I think those of us who work in areas that aren't racially or culturally diverse or work with mostly white children and families have really struggled with anti-bias work because so many of the resources focus on race. And racism is a critical piece in this country, clearly, no matter where one lives. White children in places like Vermont are bathed in it. I just have to look at my own experience to know why it's important to help white children in places like Vermont understand racism. Rural Vermonters are my people, and I don't want them to grow up ignorant the way I did. We all deserve to be given the information and the skills to work with one another toward justice, toward our dreams, and the knowledge to be allies for one another.

I believe that we need to pay attention to undoing racism and helping white children recognize the ways in which the racism around them affects their perception, whether they know people of color or not. In the classroom we do this in lots of ways, beginning with the environment—the pictures we have on the wall, the stories we think are important to tell and the perspective we tell them from, the books we read, the baby dolls, the colors of paint and playdough we use, the people we invite in or go to visit, and so forth. Many times, though, I think teachers in homogeneous settings, like most of Vermont, think that they have to *begin* anti-bias work by focusing on race because that's where so many of the resources begin, with race and color and culture. So often, despite the best intentions of the teacher, this becomes touristy because it isn't based in the children's or the teachers' knowledge or in the knowledge and daily experience of the families and communities. In addition, it neglects other pressing issues of bias the children bring with them to the classroom. In my experience, the most powerful place to begin anti-bias work is with children's real experiences and conflicts with each other and with other people in their daily lives, and in places like Vermont, those immediate, daily experiences and conflicts are often not primarily about race or culture.

After three years at Worcester Child Care I became the first director at the on-site child care center at the Waterbury factory of Ben & Jerry's Homemade Inc. Again, that was a whole new role for me because I had always worked directly with children. I had never supervised such a big staff—ten people, which seemed enormous to me! Nor had I developed an infant/toddler program or worked within the structure of a company like Ben & Jerry's. The early days of the center were very chaotic. I really had no idea how to bring a group of staff members together, or even how to begin talking about developing a shared philosophy. I knew that I would have to think about making anti-bias happen in a different way, since I wouldn't be working with the children, and I felt completely overwhelmed by the idea of trying to do that along with everything else involved in getting a new center off the ground. By this time I had read *Anti-Bias Curriculum: Tools for Empowering Young Children,* so at least I had a name for what I was trying to do. But I still felt incompetent at it, and I only knew one other director who was even familiar with the term. I didn't talk about it with staff members as I hired them because I didn't know how to. I guess I thought we would put the program in place and kind of add anti-bias thinking on top (hah!).

About two months after we opened the center, one of the teachers, Amy Brandt, came to me and said, "Well, I think I might have really blown it. I just want you to know what I did, because I have a feeling you're going to hear about this from some of the parents." There had been an ongoing interest in "getting married" in the preschool for a couple of weeks. Kids would get all dressed up in fancy clothes and talk about it. It seemed to all of us that the play was largely not about marriage

or, certainly, sexuality, but about who they could love and what love was. On this day, two four-year-old girls, who were very close friends, had gotten all dressed up and said they were going to get married to each other. One of the boys overheard them and said, in horror and disbelief, "You can't do that! Only boys can marry girls." Amy told the kids, "When you grow up you can love and live with anybody you want, and it's okay for two girls to play getting married here at school if they want to." Then she came to tell me about it, partly I think for reassurance that she had done the right thing, and partly because she knew that the incident would raise issues for parents. And it sure did! The boy's parents were at my door the next morning.

They were very upset. They belonged to a fundamentalist Christian church, and they didn't want their son to think that same-sex partners were even possible. I explained to them why Amy had responded the way she did, and I said that I supported her. Those parents pulled their kid out of the center. That night we had a staff meeting, and I said to the staff, "I have to tell you that I think Amy did exactly the right thing in this situation, and this is why." That was probably the first time I had ever used the word *anti-bias* with the staff. Well, the next thing I knew I had two staff members in my office resigning, and another family left the next week. So we lost two families and two staff members in the space of two weeks. It was quite an upheaval, and that was how we began the conversation around anti-bias work with kids. I would never choose to do it the same way again!

On the other hand, one of the parents, a local kindergarten teacher, came flying into my office the day after it all began. Wham! She slammed the door and sat down, saying, "I was at volleyball last night, and everybody was talking about the Children's Center, that you're teaching kids to be homosexual. What's going on?" So I told her the story and explained why we had reacted the way we did. I was braced for her to shake her head and say she was considering taking her kid out too. Instead she looked me straight in the eye and said, "Well, I certainly don't see a problem with that." She stood up to go and was halfway out the door when she turned around and said, "If some people don't want their kids to know anything about the world, maybe they should just keep them in a closet 'til they grow up." Wham! And out she went.

In some ways, I think I came at the anti-bias approach entirely backwards at the Children's Center. I had such clear convictions and I was so passionate about the whole thing that I don't think I gave either staff members or parents very much room to be doubtful or to process in their own ways. I didn't really have the skills to explore the issues with parents or with teachers. It was not a question to me of what parents wanted or what teachers thought was appropriate. It was a matter of doing it because it was the right thing to do, whether people agreed with me or not. And some of the things that came of that conviction were good. The center was made accessible to people with disabilities, which was not part of the original renovation plan; we created a fee scale based on everyone paying a flat percentage of their family income, up to the true cost of care; staff were put on the same pay schedule and had the same benefits as other Ben & Jerry's employees. But there was also a lot of contention, and many people left the center who I think could have been engaged in the conversation. It was good to have someone out front with the torch, but I wish I had had more knowledge of community-building and conflict management so I could have kept from burning the building down at the same time.

For example, the center opened in September, and the whole issue of holidays came up almost right away. Because I had many Jewish friends and a cousin who was a Jehovah's Witness, I knew that the assumption that everyone celebrates

Christian holidays was false. I also knew how difficult and painful the issue of holidays was for many of my Jewish friends who had children in the public schools, where Christian holidays were generally celebrated as a matter of course. I had such clear memories of elementary school and the one Jehovah's Witness kid who was always absent on the day we were having holiday parties, or who sat in a corner doing homework while the rest of the class was making valentines. That kind of exclusion just wasn't okay with me. Also, my Jehovah's Witness cousin told me that she didn't go back to work until both her kids were public school age because she knew the kind of hell their lives were going to be at school around holidays, and she couldn't bear the thought of that starting earlier if she put them in day care. I felt a responsibility to do something about that, to have our center be at least one safe place for those kids and families. No matter what our group of families was like at any given time, I wanted us always to be inviting to many different kinds of families.

I also didn't want the children in the center to get the message that Christian holidays were the norm, and anything else was an exception. I knew that our group of families and staff members was pretty homogeneous—the vast majority were European American and culturally Christian. So if we celebrated just the holidays of the cultures represented among the children, we'd end up celebrating Christian holidays. I was worried about trying to celebrate holidays for which we had no cultural background among staff or the families—our children would have no context to put these celebrations in. Plus, we didn't have the background to plan them in ways that kept them from being tourist curriculum. I had seen how many preschool programs built their curriculum around holidays, and I wanted the center's curriculum to be deeper and more connected to the children and to the natural world. So it seemed as though there wasn't a good way to celebrate holidays in the context of our program and our community.

At Worcester Child Care Center, we had a policy of not celebrating religious holidays; instead parents, children, and staff members came together three or four times a year for potluck parties. That worked pretty well, and the potlucks became shared community events in the same way that holiday parties can often bring people together. So I made the decision that we were not going to celebrate holidays at the Children's Center, and I presented this idea to staff members and then to parents. I didn't want to be a dictator—I really wanted discussion on some level—but I also had my mind made up and I think everyone knew that I just wasn't going to budge.

Now I don't think that was the most effective way to handle the situation. In fact, I hope that I would do it differently if I were doing it again. I think that the fact that I had my mind made up squelched discussion, and though that wasn't my intent, it kept people from coming together to consider the issue. It became one of Beth's Edicts that people didn't really have to understand or wrestle with because it was out of their control anyway. Now I see it as a lost opportunity for collective discussion and community-building.

Over time, as the center settled down and became known for its anti-bias approach and developed a reputation as a good place for kids and families, we attracted staff and families with similar visions. One day in our second or third year a woman dropped by with her baby. She asked to see me, and said, "I have a friend who just got your information packet. She said you have something called an anti-bias philosophy. Is that true?" I nodded, and before I could even start to explain what it was or how it affected the program, she said, "Well, I want to enroll my baby because that's what I think we need to have in the world." Like many of the parents at the center, she wasn't particularly an activist, but she was someone who cared about injustice in the world, and she wanted her child to be somewhere where he would learn about bias. As that happened more and more, it helped me to think that we were on the right track. Now I feel as though many parents are hungry for this kind of education for their children. They don't always know how to ask for it or what it will look like, and like all of us, they struggle when issues arise that are difficult for them. But they yearn for their children's education to feel real to them, to address the real experiences of their family, to deal with the real problems they see in the world around them.

With the help of staff, I also got better at hiring new staff members who were committed to the same kind of education that we were. At first, I so much wanted a diverse staff that I hired people who were too different from one another, who really didn't share many of the same values, who didn't get along with one another or with me. Then we started sending candidates a packet that included our anti-bias statement and the NAEYC anti-bias brochure. We also started doing team interviews that included at least one teacher each from the preschool and the infant/toddler program, a parent, and me. Our goal was to ask thought-provoking questions and engage the candidate in a discussion. We'd give them the questions before they came in, so they had time to reflect. We weren't looking for right answers, but to find out how people thought and how open they were. That worked amazingly well for us. If someone really wasn't with the program, it showed pretty fast.

I found that having diverse perspectives on the hiring team was crucial. I learned so much from the long discussions we'd have after a night of interviewing, and from the struggles: Was it more important to hire someone who would bring some kind of diversity to the program, someone with a background in early childhood, or someone we all warmed up to right away? It was very hard for me to give up power in that way, to let hiring be a group decision, but I learned from the times I went against the wisdom of the group that it was

always a mistake. If someone around the table had serious reservations, we were always better off heeding them, even if it meant opening up the process all over again.

Because of this, we ended up hiring people who were really committed to teaching and who shared our thinking and values about young children. Often they, like us, didn't know how to do the work they envisioned, and many times they were hoping that we could teach them. I knew we didn't have the answers they were seeking, but we could learn together. And because we were more clear about who we were and what we were looking for in the hiring process, we were better able to hire people from diverse backgrounds, support them, and challenge ourselves.

For example, at one point we started working with a substitute who was Deaf and communicated primarily through American Sign Language. We wanted Lori to be a regular part of the program because she was good with the kids, and because she brought us a needed piece of diversity. We had a child in the program that year whose parents were Deaf and whose first language was ASL. Having a Deaf teacher in the program, even part-time, validated his home language and culture and made the center a more welcoming and accessible place for his parents. We also had a summer high school intern who was Deaf.

One of our teachers was taking a morning off every week for schooling, and that gave us the opportunity to hire Lori as a regular substitute to cover that time. In order for the arrangement to work, we had to do some hard thinking about how to make the program accessible to her as a teacher. It meant some changes to the physical plant—adding flashing lights to the alarm system, making sure there was a TTY (used by Deaf people to communicate by phone) available for her to use to make phone calls and for us to use to call her. It meant staff members taking classes in ASL. It meant hiring interpreters for meetings and for my supervision with her because none of us were fluent in ASL. It meant working with a counselor from the state office of vocational rehabilitation and a Deaf ASL teacher from the University of Vermont to understand some of the cultural differences. It meant that the teachers in the preschool had to use pidgin sign with one another when they were having conversations so that she would have a sense of what was going on around her, as any of us do when we overhear one another talking in the course of the day. It meant we had to think about how to teach the children some sign and then facilitate their use of it with Lori, and also how to get the children to respond to her use of sign with them, to see her as a "real teacher." It was really a lesson for us about cultural difference and about incorporating a second language into the classroom.

It would have been easy to say, "This is just too hard," and look at how Lori didn't function in the ways that we expected substitutes to function because of the communication barrier. We could never have done it in the early years of the program—

it would have been too big a challenge. But the preschool teachers were completely committed to making it work. For the larger goal of having Lori in the program and the richness she brought with her, we had to sacrifice some smoothness and comfort. As anyone who has ever worked in child care knows, there are many days when giving up even a little comfort makes a significant difference in how manageable everyone's job feels and how smoothly the day goes for the children! We experienced a number of setbacks and miscommunication, and I don't know that it ever worked smoothly, but we all gradually got better at working together. By the end of the year we saw some real changes in the children, a number of whom started using some sign and treating Lori like a "real" teacher. More important, we succeeded in making the center more diverse and a more welcoming place for people from the Deaf community.

I also had to learn to examine and question my own values about class. Most of the staff at the Children's Center were middle class, but several came from working class backgrounds. When I thought about how I supervised one teacher, Stephanie, I realized that I didn't always value the things she did well. Because I am middle class, brought up in an academic and intellectual household, I think I tend to value certain ways of thinking and talking about work with children. I know I value the ability to conceptualize the work we do, to put it in a framework and generalize from it. Stephanie was unbelievably steady, incredibly loving, and nurturing of the children. She was tremendously reliable with parents and knew the children well. She absorbed all the anti-bias conversations and the emergent curriculum information. But she just wasn't interested in planning in that formal kind of way. For a long time I felt that meant she was deficient and it was something I had to help her do better. In my last year at the Children's Center I could finally say, "Who cares? Stephanie is an excellent scaffolder of kids' play. She is terrific at getting and keeping children involved and extending their play. She's great with parents and she's extremely practical." There were other people on staff whose strength was planning the environment or leading discussions—we didn't need everyone to be good at the same things. In fact, it was a blessing that we had her strengths to rely on. Though I don't have my finger on it exactly, I can admit that my limited view had to do with class, and I know that I have to pay attention to seeing and valuing diverse contributions.

In the end, for me, anti-bias work is about wholeness. It allows me to be the same person at work every day that I am at home, to keep intact the fabric of my convictions about children, equity, and social justice. It demands that I bring all of me to my work every day, including my thinking about social justice. Anti-bias work has enabled me to reclaim my vision of child care and education as empowerment, as a vehicle for changing the world. I feel confident in saying that—it *is* about changing the world. Our work as teachers has that kind of power. Anti-bias work provides a vehicle for not just acknowledging that power, but claiming it and using it to build in our classrooms and centers the kinds of communities we want to live in, models of the world we envision.

Discussion Questions

1. Beth speaks about working with children and families in a homogeneously white environment where the diversity in the group comes from class and other differences. How might you go about adding diverse ethnic experiences to the day-to-day lives of children in this type of environment?

2. Beth discusses a difference in the rural and urban meaning of gun play in children's lives. What do you think about her perspective? What is the context for guns in the lives of the children and families with whom you work or in the neighborhood or town in which you live? How might you handle issues around gun play in your teaching?

3. Beth talks about the need to begin anti-bias education with issues that are relevant to the children and families in the program. Which issue do you think is the best starting place for the program in which you work or for a program serving the children in your town or neighborhood? Why?

Barbara Yasui

Changing Awareness

*I*n a way, I'm a neophyte at this anti-bias work. I joined the Culturally Relevant Anti-Bias (CRAB) leadership group in Seattle when the project first started, and I felt way out of my league. I remember thinking, "Wow, how did I ever get involved with this group?" Since then I think I have changed and grown a lot. But the group members still feel like my mentors, and that can be a little bit humbling sometimes.

When I first started with the CRAB group, I was a parent educator for a local community college. I did that for five years, working indirectly with children in a cooperative preschool. In 1995 I got a part-time position as an Equity Multicultural Specialist in our public school district. So my work is mainly with adults—training and consulting with teachers and some classified employees (staff members who aren't teachers, such as bus drivers, cafeteria workers, secretaries, and educational assistants).

I was born in Portland, Oregon. I am a third-generation Japanese American. And I identify myself as Sansei, which literally means third generation. My parents were born in America, but both sets of grandparents came from Japan in the early 1900s. Though we lived in Japan for a short time when my dad was in the military, I was too young to remember. So for all intents and purposes, I grew up in the same house in Portland and stayed there until I was eighteen years old and went off to college.

I would say we were pretty middle class. Not upper, not lower, just sort of right in the middle. My father, however, was a surgeon. And so in some ways, our income was probably better than others in the neighborhood where we lived. Perhaps part of the reason we lived in that neighborhood was because my father, and especially my mother, had grown up having to make do, never having quite enough. I think this may have created a feeling of not wanting to overreach and making sure we lived where they could afford.

Because I knew about the internment so early, I think I had feelings about injustice from a very young age—that something could happen to you because of your ethnicity.

Our neighborhood was very homogeneous ethnically, almost all Euro-American. I can only remember one other family of color in my elementary school. They were African American and their house wasn't on our block, so I didn't really know them. I feel like I grew up with what one might call an all-American kind of life. I was a Campfire Girl. We celebrated Christmas, Easter, Halloween, and all those traditional American kinds of holidays. And, until high school, all of my friends were European American. My father grew up in Hood River, which is about an hour from Portland, up the Columbia River. He was one of nine children and his eldest brother had stayed on the old family farm. We would go there frequently in the summer. At holiday times other family members would gather too. That was pretty much the only time I can remember being around lots of Japanese Americans. So really there was no contact with a Japanese American community. Unlike cities like San Francisco or even Seattle, Portland didn't have a very large Japanese American population, and what it did have was pretty dispersed.

I feel like my parents really wanted us to be American, to fit in. I know that it was important to my dad that we know about the history of our family, and also about the history of Japanese Americans. From the time I was really little, he told us about the internment of Japanese Americans during World War II. My parents were interned when my dad was eighteen and my mom was about sixteen. Most third-generation Japanese Americans don't know a whole lot about the internment, but my dad wanted to make sure that we knew about it. I've since learned that this is somewhat unusual. I've been surprised to hear that parents and grandparents remain silent about the internment, because my experience was just the opposite.

Because I knew about the internment so early, I think I had feelings about injustice from a very young age—that something could happen to you because of your ethnicity. As a child, I probably thought about this only in terms of my own personal ethnicity. I can remember that in grade school the most typical taunt would be using your fingers to slant your eyes up and then down and chant about "Chinese, Japanese, Americanese." I remember it so clearly, knowing that those kinds of comments were made to me because of my ethnicity. I don't know when I realized that it happened to other people too, but I have a hunch that I was probably pretty young.

Even though our family did the traditional American cultural things, we also had a lot of Japanese American customs. We would go mushroom hunting every fall, and I'd always take a ribbing from my friends. They'd say, "Mushroom hunting? What kind of a gun do you use for mushroom hunting?" or "Do you need a license for mushroom hunting?" We also ate rice with every meal. Even if we were having spaghetti for dinner, we'd have rice too. So I would say I grew up a bicultural person, with elements of both Japanese and American culture.

I'm the eldest of three. I have a younger sister and a younger brother. For some reason, I have a stronger cultural identity than either of them, though I'm not sure why. It might just be my personality. It might be because I was the first born and so people told me more. I remember always liking show-

and-tell at school. I never hesitated to bring something from my culture. One New Year's I brought rice cakes, which are called mochi. My sister would never have done something like this. I also remember bringing leftovers for lunch, often Japanese food. My sister would get so upset. She would say, "If they see you eating that, then they'll know that I eat that too." She used to be embarrassed when Mom would come to school, but I can't ever remember feeling that way. Looking back, I think what she felt was just part of growing up—you really want to fit in and be accepted, and you don't want to be perceived as being different. She's changed now and feels comfortable with being Japanese American.

I was first around large numbers of Asian Americans when I went away to college. It was the 1970s, the height of the civil rights and anti-war movements. And though an elitist kind of school, Stanford had a lot of Asian Americans. At that time, most of the students of color were organizing into affinity groups, and I was very involved with the Asian movement. I liked being around other Asian Americans and got more and more involved. There were some anti-war components involved because of the Vietnam War, but mainly it had to do with being able to identify with other Asian American students. A dorm was established where half of the students were Asian American, and I lived there for two years, first as a resident and then as a resident advisor. I was also involved in an Asian women's group. We started a teahouse on campus—The People's Teahouse—where we would sell noodles and char siu bao (a Chinese barbecued pork bun). All the proceeds would go back to the community. College was a wonderful experience, and in many ways, it was my big awakening.

I did not experience a lot of discrimination before I went off to college, but this was the time when I became acutely aware of the discrimination that my people had suffered—especially during World War II and the internment. I also became somewhat aware of what was going on with the Vietnam War—how most Americans perceived Asians as almost subhuman or not really people at all. I could also see that it didn't matter to many people whether they were talking about Vietnamese or Japanese Americans because most weren't able to tell the difference. So if they were saying awful things about Vietnamese, they probably meant me too.

The women's movement was growing at the time, and I became aware of stereotypes about Asian women that I really didn't like. I was a psychology major and had been required to take child development. I really liked it, and the professor was wonderful. But I didn't apply any of my new awarenesses of racism and sexism to my early childhood practices or thinking. They were separate, and it wasn't until I was in graduate school that I started to see how they could come together.

I also remember bringing leftovers for lunch, often Japanese food. My sister would get so upset. She would say, "If they see you eating that, then they'll know that I eat that too."

By the time I graduated, I was feeling more Asian than American. I had studied Japanese and very much wanted to go to Japan to experience living there, so I got a job teaching English as a second language in a Japanese preschool. I was there for about eight months, and though I loved it, it made me realize how American I was.

I came back to graduate school—Oregon State University, a small town school, not very diverse. So I transferred to the University of Washington, which was much more diverse, and got my master's in early childhood education. During that time I really started to put multicultural and early childhood education together. I was a teaching assistant for the Asian American Studies Department and took as many classes as I could in multicultural education. That was the late 1970s and James Banks, who wrote a number of books on multicultural education, was in the School of Education, so I was able to take a couple of courses from him. With the multicultural education program just starting at the university, it was a great time to be there, when and where it was all happening. Then I did a practicum with the Seattle School District, where they had something called The Rainbow Program. My courses and my work with the Rainbow Program seemed like a good match, blending my interest in Japanese culture with my interest in early childhood education. As part of my practicum, I went around to various schools, practicing my multicultural lessons on kids. It was so touristy. I look back now and I think, "Oh man, I can't believe I did that!" We sang little superficial songs, counted in different languages, and did cutesy little art and holiday projects. No one was really doing anything else.

My husband isn't Asian, but he grew up near Chinatown in San Francisco. He had gone to public schools (which were 50 percent or more Chinese) before we met at Stanford, so he was very comfortable being around Asians. When we both finished graduate school, I put multicultural education and early childhood education on a back burner and we went to Japan to live for a year and a half. It seemed like a good time to go. We were recently married but had no jobs, no children, and no responsibilities, and we both wanted to experience living in another culture. We had both been to Japan in college, and we both wanted to go back. When we came back to the United States, we moved to a very, very small logging town that was almost all European American. I taught at a co-op preschool for three years. I can't remember having any children of color. I would do some of the multicultural stuff that I had done in graduate school, but I just wasn't very fired up about it. I do remember writing a letter to the superintendent asking about multicultural education. His reply was something like, "Why would we need that here?"

My daughter was about one year old when we moved to Marysville, Washington. I wanted to try running my own business, which was a very new thing for me. We bought a Gymboree franchise, did that for seven years, and lost our shirts. During that whole period, I don't think I gave multicultural anything a thought—we were just trying to survive and parent our kids.

In Washington state, all of the community colleges run independent, cooperative preschool programs. Parents get credit by helping out in the classroom and participating in a parent-education program run by the college. So the schools are for the children, but they are also for the parents. I had been a lab teacher for one of these schools, and because I liked the idea of so much parent involvement, I enrolled both my kids. After I sold my business, I decided that what I really wanted to do was early childhood education. So I got a job with Everett Community College, teaching early childhood education. Most of the students were Euro-Americans. Every quarter there may have been one or two people of color and a man or two involved, so it wasn't very diverse in those ways. But there was quite a bit of class and age diversity—from eighteen year olds fresh out of high school to people in their forties, fifties, and older coming back to school for second careers.

I joined WAEYC (Washington Association for the Education of Young Children) and NAEYC (National Association for the Education of Young Children) and started getting the newsletter. That's where I saw the announcement about the CRAB project. I remember clearly feeling that this was something I had to do. I think the feeling came both from some long forgotten part of my past and because having children of my own had really made me more and more concerned about the community we were living in and people's attitudes.

I still have that announcement. Interestingly enough, there wasn't anything particularly inspirational to it. It just said that a three-year project, headed by Louise Derman-Sparks and funded through the Kellogg Foundation, would train early childhood people in anti-bias practices. I had never heard of Louise. I had never seen the book *Anti-Bias Curriculum*. And I didn't know anyone else who was doing anti-bias education. But a little lightbulb came on in my head: This is what you have to do. I sent off the application and was so excited to be selected—until the first meeting. And then I had an overwhelming sense of "Whoa! I'm way out of my depth here!" Most of the people knew each other. Most were from another county. Plus, there was a really strong Pacific Oaks College connection that I didn't understand at all, until two or three meetings later. I would hear people saying "PO this" and "PO that." I felt like everyone was speaking a language I didn't understand. Although I really felt out of place for the first few meetings, I also felt warmly accepted and supported. From the beginning, it was an incredible experience and very, very intense.

When I did parent education, eventually even general topics included cultural and sensitivity issues and multicultural and anti-bias considerations.

The group, and my work in it, certainly influenced my job. When I did parent education, eventually even general topics included cultural and sensitivity issues and multicultural and anti-bias considerations. For instance, during a discussion about sleeping patterns, I would explain that it was important to remember that certain suggestions that might seem obvious or logical all come from a European American, dominant culture position. For example, putting the baby in its own room to prevent her from waking up in the middle of the night, putting a child on some sort of a schedule as a way of getting him to go to bed, or letting a child cry until she falls asleep. Although these procedures may be the way most Americans would handle the situation, people from other cultures might have an entirely different perspective. In many cultures there would be no question of what to do because the baby wouldn't be sleeping in a separate room. In Japan, for instance, the baby would be sleeping with the mother in the mother's bed. Or in some cultures, the whole family would be sleeping together in the same bed. So I would try to bring in those perspectives, helping parents realize that there were many different ways to approach the same issue. I knew this was important, even though my classes were not all that diverse.

Literature became another way to involve anti-bias education in my work. When I'd do a session on reading to kids and choosing appropriate books, I'd bring in multicultural or anti-bias books and interweave them into the topic. Occasionally I'd get specific: how to talk to your children about differences, how children develop racial awareness and identity. But more often than not, I would take a general parent education topic and integrate anti-bias concepts into it.

Sometimes I would sense a growth in awareness. For instance, when I talked about how children are aware of racial differences very early, someone would say, "I don't really think my child notices," or "I don't remember noticing that myself until I was much older." But the next week, or later on, a parent would come back and say, "Oh, wow! My son pointed out a person with a disability yesterday." People were paying attention, though I didn't see awareness translated into a lot of action.

Because these classes also served as a parent support group, we spent a lot of time problem solving and built up pretty solid relationships. By and large, people would at least listen politely to what I had to say. They may well have had opposite opinions, but I can't remember anybody directly challenging me about anything having to do with the importance of talking to kids about differences or the need to address these issues with children. At the same time, I think the other parent instructors in my department saw me as the "multicultural person." If we were deciding which topics to talk to parents about or what we needed to do an in-service on, they'd think, "Oh, Barb's here so we better...." Even so, at least they were doing something they might not have done before. I am sure that there were times when they didn't think the issues I valued were important or didn't agree that anti-bias education should be integrated into everything. But they didn't say so, and they didn't confront me directly, perhaps because multicultural/anti-bias work is "politically correct," and by criticizing, they risked appearing racist or biased. That's a whole other drawback to this work—I think, in some ways, it intimidates people.

Besides supporting me in all of this, the CRAB group pushed me to do things that I never, ever would have done. What I'm doing, I owe to them. I wouldn't be here now without those people encouraging me to take risks that I never would have taken otherwise. For instance, I had never really done any kind of trainings. I was very comfortable doing my little half-hour to an hour presentations on discipline or toilet training, but I had never been the trainer for two or three hours. The first time I did that, I was scared to death.

I remember that WAEYC was asking for conference proposals, so the CRAB group decided to offer a training. One of our goals was to influence WAEYC by getting our members elected as officers. Another goal was to offer a CRAB track at their conference. So this was our way to begin. When the group pushed me to be one of the trainers, I could only say that I didn't want to, that I wasn't ready. They told me I was. With their encouragement, it was still scary, but it was wonderful too. We did a panel—five of us—and gave one another so much support. That was a major boost to my confidence, and I still remember reflecting afterwards: I can do this.

The next big push for me was to teach a community college class called "Family Culture and Self-Concept." Going from little discussions once a week to ten or twelve weeks of classes felt like a very frightening step. But a colleague of mine, Louise Vlasic, the only tenured person in the Early Childhood Education Department at Everett Community College, was committed to including anti-bias curriculum in the early childhood courses. She had gone to Pacific Oaks and knew a lot of the CRAB group members, so when she asked me to teach the class with her, I was scared, but I decided to try.

As I've been doing this work, I've found that most of the resistance I've met has been my own—feeling uncomfortable, feeling like I wasn't ready. There were so many times I would think: God, why did I say I would do that? But I would go ahead, and for the most part, it would turn out fine. I'd be glad that I took the chance. All along, the key for me has been support. Of course, there have been challenges—people who I

> *As I've been doing this work, I've found that most of the resistance I've met has been my own—feeling uncomfortable, feeling like I wasn't ready. There were so many times I would think: God, why did I say I would do that? But I would go ahead, and for the most part, it would turn out fine. I'd be glad that I took the chance.*

really thought would be supportive and weren't. But I get a lot of support from CRAB members. I'm also a trainer for a group called REACH (Respecting Ethnic and Cultural Heritage). Other trainers in that group are really supportive too, and so is my colleague at Everett Community College, Louise Vlasic. I also share my job at the school district with my friend Karyn Zigler. That means there are two of us to take the heat and the criticism, which makes it a lot easier to deal with the setbacks. When I get discouraged, I always know there's someone there.

Many of our community college students have gone through some really tough experiences in their lives—losing jobs and having to find new careers; divorcing, which for many women has meant getting an education and finding a job. When you've been in those kinds of positions, it's difficult to think of yourself as privileged.

One of my biggest concerns, on a national level, is the white backlash that seems to be engulfing our society and becoming legitimized through legislation—anti-immigration, anti-affirmative action, English-only legislation, anti-gay sentiment. Perhaps this is a measure of our progress on anti-bias issues—the privileged system is being threatened. But the consequences could be disastrous.

What still confounds me the most is that many European Americans don't think anti-bias issues are important for them. That attitude has been a real obstacle. In fact, my job-share partner and I are perceived as one-issue, one-dimensional people—the Multicultural Watchdogs. I know I'm much more than that, and so is she. But the hardest thing to do is change those attitudes and convince people that anti-bias issues are important for everyone.

Another challenge in the training we do has been the whole issue of privilege, especially for the people in our community college classes. Many of our community college students have gone through some really tough experiences in their lives—losing jobs and having to find new careers; divorcing, which for many women has meant getting an education and finding a job. When you've been in those kinds of positions, it's difficult to think of yourself as privileged.

But we keep trying, and I think we've done some really good interactive work. Many of our ideas are taken from conversations with Margie Carter and Deb Curtis, who wrote *Training Teachers*. In one very effective activity, we make up about five personas with different characteristics. Each student is assigned a persona and asked to imagine that they are that person during a shopping trip. We don't ask them to act out the person, just think about their experience in the store from that perspective. We send them to a grocery store and a variety store that are right across the street from Everett Community College. They go in groups of about three or four during class time. We give them a question sheet, with questions like, "Do you see yourself represented in the advertisements?" "Do the people speak your language?" and "Is it easy for you to reach the things you need?" We ask them to pay particular attention to any situations their "new identity" creates, along with reactions from the people they come into contact with. Students always come back with comments like, "Wow, I never saw it that way before." Through activities like this, many have experienced not being in a position of privilege. Then they can speak from the heart.

The changes they've experienced have been mainly in terms of awareness. Still, there is more to do, particularly around gay and lesbian issues. I know our students are uncomfortable when that particular topic comes up in class. I can sense it. But most don't feel comfortable confronting an instructor, perhaps because we've made our stand so clear: Our commitment to taking action to stop bias and discrimination demands that we be inclusive. To be inclusive, we can't leave out sexual orientation. So students may feel intimidated, less brave about challenging us.

In every class, there've been at least one or two students who have said, for religious reasons, that there's just no way they can accept homosexuality. We've responded that they are

certainly entitled to that belief and let it go at that, or we re-iterate that it's our obligation to support all families and all children. We haven't required students to take a position. And even though we can tell they are uncomfortable from their body language or a few quietly expressed feelings, I can't ever remember a big confrontation in class.

*L*ooking back, I feel best about the work I have done with the school district. It began when my eldest child was about to start kindergarten. I wrote a letter to the superintendent explaining that my child was biracial and I was very concerned about how she was going to be treated. I asked what kinds of things were being done to make her feel comfortable. Were there any multicultural or anti-bias programs? I got a letter back saying, "No, we don't have anything and we don't really need anything. We have a few Native American students, but they have their own counselors out on the reservation, so we're fine." It was really disappointing.

So I got involved with the district as a parent volunteer. At the time, the district was working on a five-year strategic plan—from 1995 to 2000. I really pushed them to include a strong anti-bias piece. I worked with an African American friend, the same woman I now share my job with. The two of us were not going to be quiet. We convinced the superintendent to form a task force.

Then twenty-five of us spent about eighteen months writing a vision statement and plan that covered hiring and recruitment, curriculum, staff development, community involvement, education, policies, and procedures. It was adopted in 1995 and, as a result, the position of Equity/Multicultural Education Specialist was created.

Getting challenged more about anti-bias issues may mean we have more clout, or at least we are being perceived that way. Otherwise people wouldn't be so scared.

That was four years ago. Now I am one of the specialists in charge of implementing that plan. I feel good about how far the district has come. And it certainly hasn't been only because of me. There are many people who worked very hard. And though it's been a huge accomplishment, I know there's a long way to go. I have seen how seemingly immovable large institutions are. Yet I feel that if we stick together and work long enough and hard enough, we can make things change.

But just as my partner and I have more and more allies within the district, we also have more and more challenges. As our visibility increases, the number of people who are alarmed about what we're doing increases. That may not be all bad. Getting challenged more about anti-bias issues may mean we have more clout, or at least we are being perceived that way. Otherwise people wouldn't be so scared. Most of the resistance and opposition—some organized, some not—has been around the issue of sexual orientation. That was true when we were writing our vision statement, and it remains the biggest issue today.

I have always felt strongly that we have to address sexual orientation in staff development, in hiring, and in curriculum. After all, if we are going to talk about diversity and differences, if we are really going to be inclusive, we can't leave out people who are gay and lesbian. Back during our planning stages, the district had a general nondiscrimination statement, but it didn't specifically mention sexual orientation. So every time an AIDS curriculum was mandated by the state, or a proposal came up to adopt a book or a video that had anything to do with sexual orientation, organized opposition would speak out: "We don't want this taught in our schools." Fortunately, in our vision statement there's a general statement about valuing diversity and differences. But there was dissension within the group about whether to name specific kinds of diversity, and there was criticism from outside. And there is still a lot of controversy. People who in every other way say they support what we're doing will not join us on addressing sexual orientation.

I don't want to label the opposition. I don't want to say they're conservative Christian, far right politically, or any group in particular. But there is a certain segment of the community who, whether for religious beliefs or other reasons, feels that the hidden agenda of multicultural and anti-bias education is to promote being gay and lesbian. These people always have their antenna out. Any kind of program we put together—whether it be for Martin Luther King Day, a curriculum class, or a staff training—they're waiting to hear if we're going to talk about sexual orientation. This is a big challenge, and one that can cause people who would otherwise be supporters to back off. To these people, dealing with sexual orientation would create such an uproar that we wouldn't be able to proceed with some of the other goals. I've heard people say,

"Let's back down on this one thing and make everybody feel good. Then we can go on with our work."

At the same time, we also have a lot of passive resistance from teachers and administrators. They just don't participate. If we decide to have a class or a training, they won't come. After all, participation isn't required, and lack of participation is a kind of sabotage. Sometimes I wish it were mandatory. But then again, if you force people, they're going to fight you every step of the way. However, if we don't make it mandatory, we're always going to be preaching to the choir. And I can't help but ask where the institution is in all of this. The district makes

sexual harassment training mandatory. They make CPR training mandatory. So why not cultural sensitivity training?

Part of our response has been to form a multicultural committee, which meets monthly. At first, anyone could come.
Then it became institutionalized so that every school was
required to send a representative. Now we're a step further—the
school district pays each committee member a stipend. The
stipend was an interesting addition. We really fought for it, feeling like it would help to legitimize us. However, now that we
have it, we're faced with the question of whether people may be
in the group for the stipend and not because of their commitment. There are always new problems when things change.

The group is very interesting. There are teachers who have
had lots and lots of experience and have been doing anti-bias
work for a long time, and there are teachers who probably didn't
realize what they were getting into. We have a wonderful time
together, and it's been great for bringing people along. In
building the group, our whole approach was different than the
one people were used to. The district's central office had
always dictated what the schools were to do. Rather than keep
that process, we decided to identify key people in each building who believed in multicultural/anti-bias education but may
not have been feeling like they had any support. Those would
be our members, and the group's role would be to provide
them with support so they could go back into their buildings—where they were already accepted and not viewed with
suspicion—and involve others. This was a total change in the
strategy of how to deliver services.

One person in that monthly group stands out in my
mind. She's Sansei, like I am, and grew up in the Japanese
American community in Seattle. She's an educational assistant, and we were looking for classified representation. (We
don't have a whole lot of classified employees of color in the
district or in the group.) When she was asked to be in the
group, she wasn't sure about what we expected, and I think she
was a little fearful.

Every month we spend time sharing the personal stories of our own journeys. After we had done this two or three times, we asked her if she would share her story at the next meeting. She said she didn't think she had anything to say, but agreed anyway. When that meeting came, she told an incredible story about her family's attempts to assimilate. She talked about being in high school and trying to do 100 percent American kinds of things, which really struck me because she grew up in a much more ethnic community than I did, yet there was still this very strong push to assimilate. She said she had never felt Japanese American. It was something she just didn't think about. She told us of her family's silence about the internment and how she had just begun to realize, as an adult, all the pain that had come with that discovery.

I think this experience opened a kind of door for her. She now attends every training she can and goes back to her co-workers full of suggestions. In fact, she's become a real activist, eager and enthusiastic. Seeing that sort of change has been wonderful. And she's working in a school where there are at least three or four other committed people, so they have their own support network.

As long as the students of color had been quiet or, in their eyes, not causing any trouble, the administration was willing to let all the name-calling and harassment take place. But as soon as they began to assert themselves, the administration decided there was a problem.

Another approach was to offer trainings that would meet specific needs. For instance, if a school is having a problem with racial name-calling, we go to that school and deliver the training. Another example of training that meets specific needs is our work involving people from an American Indian reservation that is part of the school district, the Tulalip Tribes. Historically, our district has had really poor relations with the Tulalip Tribes. There are a lot of reasons for this, going way back to the fact that government officials used to kidnap Indian children out of their homes and send them away to boarding schools. We now offer classes on how to integrate the Tulalip history and culture into the district's social studies or literature curriculum. We may get twenty people out of one thousand to sign up, but again, our strategy is to start with a small committed nucleus of people, giving them the resources and the skills to go back to their buildings and model practices that will be attractive to other teachers. Next time, maybe twenty more people will come.

We've had a much harder time with the issues of hiring, recruitment, and policies and procedures. We've got to do a better job—especially with policies and procedures, because if they aren't in place, then nothing's really institutionalized. These are big challenges.

It's essential to have support—to know that once a month I can go to a meeting with people who care about what I'm doing, who will always be there if I need advice on a problem or just need to talk. I don't see how you could do this work any other way.

Sometimes I am left with feelings of frustration, hurt, and anger. Just recently, my partner and I were called in to try to mediate an incident at the high school. A group of European American students were distributing racist cartoons, calling the students of color names, and really intimidating and harassing them. The students of color had repeatedly turned to the administration and the teachers for help, with no response. They finally decided they weren't going to take it anymore, so they banded together to protect one another in various situations, such as getting off the bus and going to classes. As soon as they did that, they were perceived as being a threat, as if they were going to start a riot. It was at that point that the high school called us in. As long as the students of color had been quiet or, in their eyes, not causing any trouble, the administration was willing to let all the name-calling and harassment take place. But as soon as they began to assert themselves, the administration decided there was a problem.

Just talking to the students of color was so depressing. Every day they had to face being called all kinds of names, watch these terrible cartoons being circulated, and know there were teachers all around them doing nothing. We were witness to all the hurt, total frustration, and hopelessness, which was culminating in their feeling like they had nothing to lose. They felt their only alternative was to band together and fight back.

Eventually two of the European Americans were expelled. But the students of color still felt very threatened and intimidated, so they stayed organized, saying they were going to get anybody who continued to mess with them. Part of our job was to explain that resorting to violence or verbal intimidation would result in expulsion. But, at the same time, we understood why they felt the way they did. We explained this to the administration, and they responded that all of this was happening because the students of color were banding together. In other words, blaming the victims. Though not surprising, it was very discouraging.

The high school has a zero-tolerance policy for disrespect, but because it obviously wasn't being enforced, we offered to talk to the staff. The administration declined, saying the teachers were all aware of the policy. We didn't know if it was denial, cover up, or fear. We reported what had happened and offered our suggestions to the superintendent, since he was the one who originally got us involved. At that point, the principal of the high school got really upset, telling us that we had no business going over his head to his boss without consulting him first.

We've also gotten calls from elementary schools where African American girls were being called names. And the same thing was happening to a Hispanic student at another school. In truth, it's rampant throughout the entire district. And by and large, nothing's being done until it gets to the point where somebody might get hurt or there's about to be a big confrontation. As with the high school, we have tried to intervene and gotten reprimanded, accused of only seeing the side of the students of color.

Sometimes hearing these heartbreaking stories makes the two of us realize that we've just put a tiny little Band-Aid on things. And there's so much more to do with institutional racism and attitudes, so much more to work on. So we continue to use each other to keep going. That's why I think job-sharing is the answer. Of course, we also disagree sometimes, but that's beneficial in the long run because it forces us to think about our individual positions. We each have to be so clear in order to reach a compromise or resolve the disagreement.

As I've mentioned, the CRAB group has also been an incredible source of support. Our focus isn't as sharp as when we started three or four years ago. To me it feels more like a support group than an action group. We were going to do a big action piece together but it's become nearly impossible because we're all so overcommitted in our other jobs. We do have a training piece in each meeting that is very helpful. And we still do workshops with one another. But most of all, the support is just great. It's essential to have support—to know that once a month I can go to a meeting with people who care about what I'm doing, who will always be there if I need advice on a problem or just need to talk. I don't see how you could do this work any other way.

Besides finding support, I think it's important for people starting out in this work to start small. It's so easy to get overwhelmed because there's so much to do. Sometimes it feels almost as if the work is this huge octopus and you don't know where to grab on. So, to me, another key is to start with something you know you can be successful at and then take it one little step at a time, trying not to be afraid of making mistakes along the way.

In my job with the school district, just when we seem to be making progress on one front (such as staff training), we'll hear about another incident of bias or discrimination involving kids. It often feels like we're spending all our time putting out small fires instead of dealing with how to prevent fires in the first place—being reactive instead of proactive. But it's those same incidents involving kids that keep me going. As long as children are being hurt by bias and discrimination on a daily basis, I can't stop. I have to keep reminding myself that this is a marathon, not a sprint. And I've learned that while you mustn't lose sight of the long-range goal, you've got to celebrate small accomplishments too.

It's very hard to do this work and not have it spill over into your personal life, because you get so emotionally involved. For example, I am definitely uncomfortable addressing classism. My father was a doctor and I never wanted for anything. I also married a man whose family was very well off, so I've had to struggle with my classism. I used to feel guilty about it (and sometimes still do). And I tried to keep my background of privilege a secret. But at last, now I can acknowledge it. I still take so much of my economic privilege for granted, and I'm sure that must affect my teaching. But I'm working on it, and thanks to colleagues and friends who "call" me on it all the time, I think I'm becoming more aware.

As long as children are being hurt by bias and discrimination on a daily basis, I can't stop. I have to keep reminding myself that this is a marathon, not a sprint.

Still, there is always more to learn about yourself and your assumptions. My homophobia manifests itself in a reluctance to bring up the subject when I think that it will cause problems or be controversial. I tend to back down when confronted or couch my support for gay and lesbian families in the unassailable position that "We need to support all children and their families." I know that it's the chicken way out, but it's an area that I still struggle with.

The CRAB group has also made a difference in my sense of self. My identity as an Asian American woman has been fairly strong since my college days, but I am much more aware of my position as a financially secure, able-bodied, heterosexual person than I was before I got involved with the CRAB group. Also, a new perception of myself as an agent of change has come about both because of my involvement with the CRAB group and my position with the school district. How did I become aware of these changes in myself? Through reflection and the experience of repeatedly beating my head against a brick wall, only to find that sometimes a tiny dent appears—in the wall.

At home I think that my husband and children, while very supportive, sometimes get tired of me always being on some "crusade" and wish that I would give it a rest. On the other hand, it's made all of them, especially my kids, more aware of bias and prejudice in everyday life. They often bring things up that they hear or witness at school and are quick to point out whenever someone else (including me!) is being biased or prejudging someone. I see them developing a sensitivity and awareness that I don't think I had at their age.

How did I become aware of these changes in myself? Through reflection and the experience of repeatedly beating my head against a brick wall, only to find that sometimes a tiny dent appears—in the wall.

I think that many of my longtime friends (most of whom are European American), while still supportive, see me on some multicultural mission and tend to humor me on antibias issues. However, it has made them more sensitive and aware of these issues too. I now have many more friends from diverse backgrounds than I did in my pre-CRAB days. I don't think this has been a conscious effort on my part, I just naturally come in contact with more diverse people, and some have become good friends. There's a connection with these friends that's missing with my other friends.

So what I am doing now feels like the answer to the question What do you want to be when you grow up? It feels right in so many ways. And I feel a sense of fulfillment and purpose I've never felt before. I can see myself doing anti-bias work for a very long time. There's certainly a lifetime of work to be done!

Discussion Questions

1. Barbara writes about the challenges posed by including homophobia in the list of biases to be addressed by an anti-bias approach. How do you address this in your work? Do you think it is important to include it as part of an anti-bias perspective? Why or why not?

2. Barbara raises the issue of social class, speaking of her discomfort in revealing her relative affluence. How has the issue of class affected you? Are there situations in which you're uncomfortable discussing your social class background?

3. Barbara mentions being considered the "multicultural watchdog" by some of her peers. This is not unusual. Have you experienced this? How might you help others see their responsibility to monitor the nature and success of their own anti-bias work?

Cecelia Alvarado
Louise Derman-Sparks
Patricia Ramsey

Reflecting on the Work of Anti-Bias Educators

As we read these authors' tales of their journeys with anti-bias curriculum, we saw common themes. We found that these broad themes validated the conclusions the three of us had formed over the decades of our involvement with teachers using an anti-bias approach. In this chapter we attempt to articulate those themes and to add our thoughts about the implications they might present for teachers, directors, and teacher educators who are working with an anti-bias approach in their classrooms or programs.

1 Anti-bias work is an ongoing process of self-discovery and change.

Teachers engaged in anti-bias work must investigate their own attitudes and assumptions and the early experiences that formed them. All of the authors discuss the necessity of constant self-reflection and questioning as part of the anti-bias approach. Because we live in a society whose institutions continue to be shaped by racism, classism, sexism, and other oppressions, our perception has been shaped by these issues, and we have to pay careful attention in order to notice and understand them. Anti-bias issues arise continually in our daily lives—but we must learn to see them. Most of the teachers describe the process of self-discovery and change as a lifetime journey, and would agree with Annette's comment that working on her own personal growth keeps anti-bias work alive and challenging.

All the teachers recall key childhood experiences that influenced their later commitment to justice. The pain of racism was woven into the earliest memories of the teachers of color. Consider, for example, LaVita's experiences with overt racism when she participated in a voluntary bussing program to attend a "better" predominantly white junior high school, or Linda's account of the routine humiliation of Latino children at her Catholic elementary school. The more subtle invalidation experienced by Annette, who wanted to be white as a child, and Barbara, who tried to be as "American" as possible, also reflect the racism in our society. Linda describes being ridiculed and punished for speaking Spanish and how her self-consciousness about her accent silenced her as an adult. The teachers of European American background were also affected by the biases in their surroundings. For example, Beth, whose family is middle class, was confused by the differences that she saw between her own life and those of her friends from poor and working-class backgrounds.

Each author reveals how anti-bias thinking has changed ways of behaving and thinking that stem from his or her early life. As June says, "Reflection is part of anti-bias work, and honesty has got to be a part of that reflection. So many of us have memories of racism that we've buried out of shame. In trying to understand myself and examining my memories, I have had to acknowledge parts of my life that I didn't want to remember at all." And Barbara says, "My identity as an Asian American woman has been fairly strong since my college days, but I am much more aware of my position as a financially secure, able-bodied, heterosexual person than I was before I got involved [in anti-bias work]."

Another aspect of the process of self-discovery and change is grappling with one's own discomfort or lack of confidence in speaking out and acting on anti-bias issues. As Barbara explains, "I've found that most of the resistance I've met has been my own—feeling uncomfortable, feeling like I wasn't ready. There were so many times I would think, God, why did I say I would do that? But I would go ahead, and for the most part, it would turn out fine. I'd be glad that I took the chance."

Implications for Teachers

Teachers who do anti-bias work must constantly reflect on how their responses to children, families, and fellow staff members are influenced by their own backgrounds and histories. By looking at themselves as honestly as they can and by investigating the subtle effects of racism, sexism, and other biases on their responses to themselves and other people, great strides in understanding can be made. We are not suggesting that teachers become tongue-tied or paralyzed as they analyze every gesture and word, but that they open up to feelings of discomfort or uneasiness and investigate what causes them. It is important to keep in mind that everyone goes through these trials, because we all have past experiences that have misinformed and hurt us, particularly around issues of difference. We are not responsible for these past injustices, but we are responsible for our present and future behavior and attitudes. Confronting these issues can be a source of growth, as illustrated in several of the stories.

Implications for Directors
Directors play an essential role in creating an open and supportive environment in which teachers feel safe to openly and honestly talk with colleagues about themselves. As Linda comments, learning to be honest about oneself doesn't happen all at once but takes time. Thus, directors (and teachers) should not be impatient and try to force openness before the staff has developed trusting relationships with one another. To be effective in this work, directors first need to reflect on their own lives, examine painful memories, and challenge their current assumptions and practices.

Implications for Teacher Educators
Teacher educators can include self-awareness activities in their classes and workshops. Class exercises that involve recalling and sharing childhood memories are very helpful. These formative experiences affect students' current identities, attitudes, and behaviors with people within and outside of their racial and cultural groups. As with directors, teacher educators must spend time reflecting on and challenging the attitudes and assumptions that guide the messages embedded in their pedagogy.

2 Each teacher's development as an anti-bias educator has its own pattern, pace, and timetable.

Every teacher has her or his own history, life demands, priorities, and current challenges. Thus, no two paths are alike. Recall Barbara's story of how she first became interested in multicultural work in graduate school, then put her interest on a back burner for several years, only to return to it when her children began attending school. Later, her connection with the CRAB (Culturally Relevant Anti-Bias) leadership group in Seattle inspired her to make anti-bias work her primary focus. In contrast, Eric and Beth began to address issues of diversity and social justice early in their professional careers, although it took them several years of exploration to learn how to do so.

Despite the many different entry points, all of the teachers included in the book were profoundly affected by their first encounter with the burgeoning anti-bias education movement, either in the form of the classic book on the subject, *Anti-Bias Curriculum: Tools for Empowering Young Children*, the Culturally Relevant Anti-Bias leadership groups, or Louise Derman-Sparks herself. Contributors to this book had prior professional and personal experiences that led them to question current educational practices. In many cases they felt frustrated and isolated by their concerns. When they first heard the term anti-bias or read the *Anti-Bias Curriculum* book, they felt that they were no longer alone in their struggles. Suddenly they had a peer group, a direction, and specific tools to help children learn to resist becoming either perpetrators or targets of racism and other oppressions. Linda recalls her sense of validation when she first heard a discussion of anti-bias curriculum goals by Louise Derman-Sparks at her daughter's child care center. Barbara describes reading the announcement about the formation of the CRAB group in Seattle: "A little light-bulb came on in my head: This is what you have to do." Beth describes herself as "feeling my way toward anti-bias work long before I had ever heard the word."

None of the teachers whose stories are told in this book started out with a master plan, only a general sense of the kind of work they were trying to do and the problems that they wanted to address. Even after they became involved in anti-bias work, their development was organic in the sense that their understanding and practice was shaped by encounters with children, families, and colleagues. One step led naturally to the next, often in unexpected and untried directions.

Implications for Teachers

Teachers can learn to measure their progress by assessing their own goals and growth and avoid comparing themselves to others or some ideal vision of "The Anti-Bias Teacher." Teachers must remember that anti-bias work looks different in each setting and cultural context and should not compare themselves to teachers in other places. Of course, teachers can learn from others, but as the contributors to this book learned, how they implement what they learn must be "in their own way."

Implications for Directors and Teacher Educators

It is essential that directors and teacher educators see each person as unique and not expect everyone to be on the same timetable. As Annette says, "I've learned, through a lot of mistakes, that people have to grow at their own rates and in their own ways and that no one is going to grow like me. There was a time when I wanted to force growth, a time when I felt there had to be a formula. Now I am aware that we all grow differently, and I am able to appreciate and listen to people who are at various stages of growth." Directors and teacher educators who create spaces for staff members and students to explore the contradictions in their lives and to see new possibilities are offering meaningful assistance toward resolution and understanding of very tough issues.

3 Anti-bias work reflects larger social justice issues.

Anti-bias work requires constant rethinking about the world, which is often accompanied by feelings of frustration, anxiety, pain, and anger. As Beth explains, "Work around oppressions often is confusing. It's not straightforward. It is difficult to try to untangle our visceral experiences and everything we were taught implicitly and explicitly, and then understand how all of it jibes with what we know intellectually about institutionalized oppression. The challenge is to embrace that complexity and confusion and all those feelings and work through them to some kind of inner clarity."

This challenge is vividly illustrated in several of the contributors' accounts of how they faced and dealt with the complexities of confronting homophobia. First, they had to acknowledge their fears. Linda relates that she was uncomfortable talking about homophobia when she did anti-bias presentations because she was afraid of being confronted by someone with strong opposing beliefs. She then goes on to describe her remorse when feedback from a young gay man at one of her workshops helped her realize how hurtful her silence could be: "There I was, a woman who as a young brown girl had not been validated. And I was failing to validate this man. I saw his hurt and pain." After that incident she resolved to work on what was holding her back so she could speak out. In a similar vein, Eric writes that while most of the staff at his center agree that homophobia is a bias, they had to make an effort to work against it: "It's hard to get started when you know you'll get challenged or attacked for it at just the time you're least sure of yourself....So I'm trying to clarify what's relevant to young children's lives, how to present our ideas to parents...."

Acknowledging gay rights and confronting homophobia does open up the possibility of real risks. Consider Beth's discussion of the incident in which two four-year-old girls dressed up and said they were going to get married to each other. When one of the other children insisted that only boys can marry girls, a teacher responded, "When you grow up you can love and live with anybody you want, and it's okay for two girls to play getting married here at school if they want to." Beth supported the teacher and, consequently, two families and two staff members left the center. On the other hand, Beth also reports support from other parents and staff.

In another example, Barbara explains that most of the resistance and opposition that she has experienced in her work has been around sexual orientation. Nevertheless, she makes clear that addressing sexual orientation is part of anti-bias work: "After all, if we are going to talk about diversity and differences, if we are really going to be inclusive, we can't leave out people who are gay and lesbian." Barbara stuck to her position, even though it meant controversy and even possible loss of support from some members of her district's multicultural committee.

In various ways, the seven teachers came to see the relationships between anti-bias work with children and larger social justice activism. Some began as social activists who were drawn to the field of early childhood because they saw teaching as a way to work for social change. For example, June was involved in radical politics and protest marches in the 1970s and carried that perspective into her teaching. Beth writes about an incident in the preschool where she worked after graduating from college that crystallized her thinking: "At that moment, I began to make a conscious connection between my sense that something was being overlooked in our work with children and my growing political understanding of the dynamics of oppression."

Other contributors to this book began with an interest in working with children and became more aware of the fundamental injustices in our society as they saw their effects on children and families. In some cases, they have then gone on to become activists outside of the classroom. Linda became involved with the Women's League for Peace and Freedom and the Children's Peace Camps they sponsor, Annette has begun to work with PBS television doing diversity workshops with teachers, and Barbara took on the challenge of transforming her whole school district.

Seeing their work in a larger systemic perspective helps teachers make connections among all aspects of anti-bias education. Annette mentions how learning about institutional racism was important to her reclaiming and becoming proud of her cultural identity. Beth speaks of the inspiration she gets from reading *Rethinking Schools,* a publication that addresses education in relation to fundamental social, economic, and political issues in the United States and wished that she had had that resource as a beginning teacher.

Implications for Teachers

Awareness of local and national social, political, and economic environments is a critical part of the necessary analysis for each anti-bias educator. This will help them see how their own lives and assumptions have been shaped and enable them to help children and parents understand the forces that are affecting their lives. Knowledge and sometimes participation in groups engaged in social change may be meaningful and an encouraging extension of anti-bias teaching.

Implications for Directors

Directors who are involved in the local community and attuned to the shifting political, economic, and social tides are a greater support to families and teachers affected by these issues. Supporting teachers who take risks and speak out (as Beth did) by devoting some time during staff meetings and in-service trainings to discussions about what is happening in the world and how that is affecting children and families is time well-spent. Directors can also help teachers and parents connect with groups engaged in similar struggles. (Explore *The Visionary Director,* by Margie Carter and Deb Curtis, for help thinking about ways to support teachers and parents in approaching such issues.)

Implications for Teacher Educators

Teacher educators can make a huge contribution to this work by encouraging prospective and in-service teachers to learn about the larger world, to take courses in economics and politics, and to develop critical thinking skills for interpreting news stories and official explanations of policies such as welfare reform and educational budget cuts. Teacher educators can put teachers in touch with groups that are trying to make a difference.

4 Meaningful anti-bias education requires a constructivist approach that is grounded in children's real experiences. Teachers must listen with openness and respect to children and their parents.

Meaningful anti-bias education begins by fostering a firm, positive identity grounded in a child's home culture. Several contributors to this book describe the complexities and dilemmas inherent in making their classrooms culturally relevant to their children. For example, June modified her classroom to reflect the cultures of the African American children but then realized that she had created an exclusionary environment for the Latino children in her class. She then had to rethink her assumptions and extend her culturally relevant approach to include a second culture. Beth's discussion of the role of hunting and guns in rural Vermont illustrates how cultural relevancy can give rise to conflicts in cultural values, even when all of the families involved are European American.

Despite these complexities, cultural relevancy is affirming and empowering to families. For example, by opening up parent group discussions to include diverse cultural perspectives, Barbara validated parents who want to raise their children in their home culture and language and gave them tools to help their children negotiate between two cultures. Annette talks about learning to pay careful attention to how her own culture affects the children's learning and interactions with her. To help her construct curriculum that is relevant to each child, she regularly asks herself questions after each day's experiences in her classroom ("What part does my culture play?" "What expectations did my parents have of school?" "Who is benefiting from this program the way it works right now?").

Teachers build their anti-bias curriculum from the issues that arise every day in the classroom. Children's interactions with one another and with adults reveal their interests and concerns and the knowledge they have learned from their families and communities. As Annette says, "If you're aware of it, diversity hits you every day." Eric's story provides many examples of how a teacher can effectively use children's interests, issues, and questions. Recall the girls in his classroom who were obsessed with fashion and female gender stereotypes. What began as a "discipline" problem turned out to have far-reaching possibilities for the exploration of gender roles. By taking the children's interests seriously, not only did Eric seize an opportunity to explore anti-bias subject matter, he succeeded in engaging children who were detached from the curriculum he had been presenting.

Another telling example of building anti-bias curriculum from everyday classroom issues is when Eric used a flannel board character's comment that "I can see the colors, but I can't tell what those pictures are about" to expand his unit on sight into a series of activities about what people use to help them see—magnifying glasses, telescopes, and binoculars—and how people who can't see negotiate their daily lives (for example, to explore reading and writing in Braille). Eric brought in Braille books and a Braille type-writer and members of the community who use canes and dog guides. On a walk around the campus, the children discovered Braille signs and campaigned to get Braille signs posted for doors that didn't have them. Annette also shares a vivid example of building on children's questions or comments when she relates the incident when two children were talking about how white people and black people talk.

Another side to building on children's experiences is illustrated by LaVita's efforts to broaden the experience of the white children in her classroom. She says, "I was determined to provide my students with experiences that showed people of color in a variety of roles. In Winnetka, most of the people of color that these white children saw were in service roles....So I exposed children to interactions with people of color in power roles as opposed to the ones they were used to seeing."

Implications for Teachers
By learning as much as they can about children's backgrounds and earlier history, as well as their families' roles and relationships in the community, teachers will gain information and perspective neces-sary for offering appropriate support and resources. Observing children's play and listening carefully to children's question and conversations with one another are also critical. Questions such as "What do you think?" and "Why do you think so?" may reveal what children are thinking and how they arrive at their conclusions.

Teachers can encourage children to comment about specific aspects of their lives by using books, pictures, persona dolls, and other materials. These materials draw children's attention to certain themes and allow the teacher to probe a little to see if the children are interested and ready to pursue them. When anti-bias issues emerge from the use of these materials, teachers can follow up on them by either extending an already existing series of activities or developing some new ones. In addition, teachers use their knowledge of children's thinking, home life, and the larger societal context to introduce activities that support the four goals of anti-bias education. For children who are from groups that are often marginalized, teachers may choose to keep the focus on those children's backgrounds.

For children who come from homes that speak languages other than English, bilingual methods that promote the continued development of the child's home language while gradually introducing them to English are integral to a culturally relevant anti-bias approach. Teachers of white middle- and upper-class children, a group who is overly represented in the media and shielded from some of the harsher realities of American society, may concentrate on presenting a more realistic image of the diversity and injustices in our country. Children from these backgrounds also benefit from learning about white people who have been or are currently part of the movements for social change and justice in our country.

Implications for Directors and Teacher Educators
Teacher educators and directors can support teachers and prospective teachers in honing their observational and conversational skills, which are so essential to working effectively with parents. In workshops and articles they can also share literature about the impact of racism and sexism on young children's development of identity and attitudes and the significance of home language and culture in early development. Work by Beverly Tatum, Lisa Delpit, Lily Wong Fillmore, Lourdes Diaz Soto, and Jim Cummins is valuable in this area. This information can help teachers anticipate and recognize children's concerns, ask better questions, and create more effective culturally relevant classrooms. Finally, teacher educators and directors can play a key role in introducing teachers to the histories of the several ethnic groups that make up the United States, and to historical and contemporary movements of resistance to social injustice.

5

As they construct anti-bias curriculum and environments, teachers must constantly reflect on their work, learn from their mistakes, and keep trying.

All of the contributors to this book describe reflecting on their work. Sometimes they do it on a day-to-day basis, as in Annette's description of the questions she regularly asks herself and writes about in her journal ("Why was it so difficult with this child? What are my feelings about this situation? What questions came up for me today?"). This regular reflection keeps Annette's attention on what is happening with her children and with herself as she deals with the issues of diversity and injustice that appear each day in her classroom. Other times the contributors take a longer look, as LaVita does when she looks back on her experiences at the Winnetka Center.

All the authors speak about mistakes that they made and how they learned from them. For example, Eric describes hearing the children's confusion after his initial lectures on sexism when one child says to one another, "Boys have penises and girls have vaginas, and that's sexism." And Beth describes the lessons she learned from the mistakes she made in her initial efforts to bring anti-bias ideas to the staff at the Ben & Jerry's child care center and then goes on to describe how she would now do it.

Along the way all of the contributors to this book learned to let go of the traditional image of a professional teacher as someone who knows all the answers. They came to realize that an early childhood professional is someone who knows how to ask questions and to learn from other people of all ages. Their recognition that there isn't a point where you feel that you know it all also freed them to keep forging ahead.

Implications for Teachers

When teachers approach this work with open minds and hearts, when they truly listen to what children and parents have to say, then they can construct the curriculum using their own insights and those that they have gained from families and children. As good constructivists, teachers can create curriculum as an experiment that they constantly monitor and adjust as they watch the children, learn new information, and deepen their understanding.

Implications for Directors

If teachers are treated as directors want them to treat children—that is, with room for experimentation, asking questions, and testing hypotheses—teachers will take risks. Directors can observe teachers or arrange for peer observations to help teachers see new possibilities in their work (for example, ways of incorporating anti-bias themes in an ongoing curriculum) that may not be obvious from their vantage point.

Implications for Teacher Educators

In the construction of their courses, teacher educators can incorporate activities that encourage and allow their students to practice being reflective about their ideas and work. They can also model through their own pedagogy how to reflect on classroom events, to critically question what they are doing, and to make changes. (See Elizabeth Jones' work on teaching adults in *Growing Teachers* and *Teaching Adults*.)

6 Anti-bias work requires acknowledging and accepting complexity.

An environment built on respect for everyone's background and needs and dedicated to eradicating discrimination is inherently complex. Beth describes the issues that arose when a staff member who was Deaf and communicated primarily through American Sign Language joined the staff. Beth had to orchestrate several key changes including adapting the physical plant and ensuring that other staff members and children learned at least some American Sign Language. As Beth wrote, "It would have been easy to say 'This is just too hard'....For the larger goal of having Lori in the program and the richness she brought with her, we had to sacrifice some smoothness and comfort....We experienced a number of setbacks and miscommunications, and I don't know that it ever worked smoothly, but we all gradually got better at working together. By the end of the year, we saw some real changes in the children...." Eric also describes the many issues and disagreements that the Cabrillo staff had to consider and work through in the process of deciding whether to initiate a bilingual program in their center. Even longtime "givens" and apparently sacred beliefs within the early childhood field are more complex and culturally determined than we realize at first. Beth describes how the role of guns and hunting in the rural culture of Vermont forced her to rethink the early childhood edict of "no gun play in the classroom." Like many other teachers of children from poor families and children of color, Beth also found that assurances such as "the police help people" rang hollow in her community. As Annette puts it, "Diversity makes you aware that things are not always as you assume. It challenges your paradigm and makes you grow." Consequently, constructing anti-bias practice in one's center or classroom does not proceed smoothly. As Eric says, "There have been so many times when I felt like I started out in one place, traveled a million miles, and then found that—Surprise!—the universe had put me right back at the beginning."

Implications for Teachers

If teachers can take the attitude that we each have limitations that are framed by our particular experience and can open up to a variety of new perspectives, learning possibilities are endless and improvement is guaranteed. We needn't fear one another's opinions, because any idea or practice challenged and tested repeatedly and revised as needed will emerge clearer and stronger in the process.

Implications for Directors

Directors can support teachers who are trying to figure out complex issues by giving them time and not forcing them to jump to quick solutions. They can listen to teachers' dilemmas and discouragement and help teachers consider their options. Especially critical is not using evaluation to stifle these explorations.

Implications for Teacher Educators

In order to prepare their students to struggle with uncertainty, teacher educators can assign readings that express divergent views on the same topic, and they can create writing assignments in which students have to struggle with different layers of meanings and opposing opinions. Class sessions might include debates and simulations that force students to experience the complexity of educational issues.

7 By embracing disagreement and conflict, teachers can enhance their anti-bias work.

Passionate disagreement and conflict about anti-bias issues are inevitable. Early childhood teachers need to pay careful attention to differences, both obvious and subtle, between themselves and other staff and between themselves and parents. Disagreements can arise over any and all aspects of teaching and children's socialization, and they often evoke conflicts within ourselves. Eric describes questioning his assumptions about core socialization values such as autonomy and independence when he engaged in dialogue with parents whose perspectives were different from his own.

We hear a lot about conflict resolution. For anti-bias work, however, the term *conflict management* may be more appropriate. As Cirecie Olatunji says in *Future Vision, Present Work* (Redleaf, 1998), this term "acknowledges that differences in perspective, tensions, and conflicts are real, inevitable, and growth producing." When confronting issues fraught with injustice and opposing perspectives, conflict may defy resolution, but it can be managed. Eric relates how he gradually comes to the conclusion that he couldn't let himself be paralyzed by fear of criticism, that he had to move ahead with his best thinking, learn from the results, listen to the criticism, and try again. June was initially devastated when an African American father at a school meeting angrily accused her of being racist. Although initially both hurt and angry, later discussion with the father helped June understand what she had done to evoke his reaction, and she realized that he had taught her a valuable lesson.

In the early childhood field, we often see a tendency to avoid confrontation and conflict, with the goal being a softer, more nurturing approach to communication and relationships. The result can be lack of clarity, repressed anger, and indirect and increasing resentment toward the person who is unable to engage in healthy debate and disagreement.

Several contributors to this book describe how they grew through facing disagreement rather than running from it. Barbara worked for several years with her district's multicultural committee, and she was faced with a variety of challenges. Yet she was able to hang in and do creative strategizing. Initially the school superintendent told her the district had no need for multicultural or anti-bias programs. Four years later, thanks to the efforts of Barbara and other parents and teachers, an equity/multicultural education specialist position was established, and Barbara got the job. She comments, "And though it's been a huge accomplishment, I know there's a long way to go....I have seen how seemingly immovable large institutions are. Yet I feel that if we stick together and work long enough and hard enough, we can make things change."

On the other hand, LaVita's account of the painful struggle she waged at her preschool illustrates that conflict can become so serious that persistence and courage are not enough, and it is necessary to move on to another place for one's own health. Her deep conviction about the need for anti-bias education and her faith supported her through situations from which many might have run right away. Even though LaVita finally left that center, however, she was able to use her experiences there to gain deeper understanding of anti-bias work.

Implications for Teachers

Many early childhood teachers are attracted to the field because they like nurturing children and families. By training and inclination, they often find it difficult to acknowledge conflicts, much less openly deal with them. Yet anti-bias work requires keen attention to differences—their subtleties, their origins, the complex motivations behind them, and the emotions surrounding them. Teachers need to learn to face conflicts and to let go of their ideals of harmonious relationships among staff and between staff and parents. Teachers can remember that equilibrium is not static, but instead implies constant motion to maintain the balance. Teachers can gain skills in managing conflict so that it is instructive rather than detrimental to their ongoing work with children and families.

Implications for Directors

Directors also need to accept the inevitability of conflict and support staff members who are in disagreement either among themselves or with parents. Directors can sometimes serve as mediators, but they also need to know when they are not effective at mediating (for example, if they are too partisan themselves or feel intimidated by those involved in the dispute). In this case they should acknowledge their limitations and consider other options for addressing the issue, such as brainstorming possible solutions, gathering more information to inform everyone involved, calling in another colleague to help, and so on.

Implications for Teacher Educators

By using strategies described in the previous section, teacher educators can help teachers and prospective teachers learn to see conflict as both inevitable and growth producing. In the safety of a classroom or workshop, teachers can learn how to separate real issues from personal reactions, and they can practice asserting themselves and raising issues in more productive ways.

8 Discussion, community-building, and conflict management among staff is integral to making anti-bias education real and relevant in each setting.

Nowhere is the willingness to live with complexity and conflict more essential than in teachers' relationships with administrators and other staff members. The need to keep everyone happy or have harmony at any price is not compatible with the strong feelings and knotty issues raised by the anti-bias curriculum. However, an autocratic approach is just as ineffective when dealing with complex issues. This pitfall is illustrated in Beth's critique of her initial approach to holidays with her staff and the families at the center. In her own words, her holiday policy became one of "Beth's Edicts," or a policy "that people didn't really have to understand or wrestle with because it was out of their control anyway." She adds, "Now I see it as a lost opportunity for collective discussion and community-building."

The work settings described in the chapters of this book fall on a continuum of supportive to hostile. Eric and Beth's work environments were the most supportive to doing anti-bias education. In both cases the center staff shared a commitment to anti-bias goals and spent considerable time discussing the issues and planning. Although staff members did not always agree with one another, they were able to talk and manage, if not resolve, conflict. As Eric explains, "We can usually talk, listen, and respect one another's efforts." He accepts that conflict is inevitable yet must not be fatal: "I have to say to myself, 'These are people whose work with children is wonderful. If I can't talk to them about tough issues, then I'm doomed, because these are my allies.'"

Barbara, Linda, and Annette's work settings fell in the middle of the supportive-hostile continuum. On the one hand, Barbara received a lot of support from some parents and teachers in the district and has been able to build a district-wide teachers anti-bias support group. However, she also faced strong disagreement, palpable disinterest, and deliberate misunderstanding of anti-bias work. Linda and Annette felt free to do what they wanted within their classrooms without interference or hostility from other staff, administrators, or parents. However, in contrast to Eric's opportunities for regular discussion and support from staff members, Linda and Annette get their primary support from colleagues and friends outside of their work environment.

June and LaVita's work environments fell on the hostile end of the continuum. June was able to do what she believed in her classroom, but she experienced a lot of anger and rejection from her colleagues. June reports, "A few years ago, several staff members told me that if I would just keep my mouth shut, there would be no racism at school. And they really believed that." She also describes a difficult interaction with a colleague and friend, which was never resolved. She was told, "June, this is all your fault. You got involved in all this anti-bias, undoing racism kind of stuff, and you want to say that we're all racist. You think your anti-bias stuff is the right way, and as long as you continue, we won't be able to be friends." June was able to continue her work but only because she had a supportive network outside of the center.

LaVita's work setting was the most difficult for implementing anti-bias teaching, or even surviving as a teacher of color. Her efforts were constantly undermined by strong and angry resistance from some parents, coupled with inadequate and ambivalent support from other staff members. Moreover, the director was unable or unwilling to provide a safe place for discussions about racism and airing of conflicts. Ultimately, these attitudes and behaviors made it impossible for LaVita to continue her work at that center.

Implications for Teachers

Anti-bias work can be done in a variety of settings. It is best when everyone is in some agreement and is able to offer one another support. However, this level of agreement is unlikely in many situations and not absolutely necessary. Recognizing, acknowledging, and managing conflicts are essential steps we must all learn because conflict will inevitably occur if people are encouraged to explore ideas and express their thoughts and feelings. Teachers can also analyze where their environments fall in the supportive-hostile continuum so that they understand better what help is available and what they are up against. If it is clear that their setting is at the hostile end or even somewhere in the middle of the continuum, they need to put their energy into finding support and advice about anti-bias work from outside of the setting.

Implication for Directors

One of the greatest gifts a director can give staff is the creation of safe places where they can express themselves openly and learn to effectively handle conflict. Directors often feel beleaguered, blamed for all the misfortunes of a program, and not appreciated for all that they do, so it is easy to get defensive and simply dismiss vocal staff members as troublemakers. Since many conflicts are between directors and teachers, directors have to know when to stop talking and promoting their point of view and when to allow and encourage open discussion among co-workers. It is definitely an advanced skill that reaps tremendous benefits if mastered.

Directors themselves need to have a support system so that they can get help in being clear about their perspective and how to express it objectively so as not to fuel the fires of conflict. Directors who take the time to analyze where their staff relations lie on the supportive-hostile continuum have taken the most important step toward resolving issues of conflict. Despite the personal pain that this scrutiny may cause, more effective action can be taken if the dynamics are seen as they are—not as we wish they were. When directors are able to honestly evaluate the environment in their programs, they are more able to see the many possible courses of action they could take to improve matters. These might include outside consultants, workshops, or retreats, just to name a few possibilities.

Implications for Teacher Educators

Illustrating the social and political realities inherent in educational institutions and systems is eye-opening and essential for the preparation of educators who will spend much of their professional life invested in them. They will gain a sense of their competence and self-worth based on the relationships they build with colleagues and students. If we leave teachers with the expectation that these relationships will always be harmonious and tranquil, we do them a disservice. By using case studies and role-playing situations regarding staff relations, teacher educators can help their students explore strategies for dealing with a wide-range of behaviors and developing competencies that build workplace support.

9 Parents play a key role in effective anti-bias education.

Families carry the primary responsibility and an ongoing role in nurturing the development of their children's healthy identity and comfort with the diversity in the human family. Moreover, because effective anti-bias education must be constructed in relation to the community contexts of each new group of children, teachers must depend on dialogue with the children's families to develop meaningful goals and activities. Consequently, anti-bias education work requires an open, collaborative relationship with families.

Annette writes about how she builds trusting relationships with the children's families from the very beginning. She rides home on the bus with the children because "seeing where they live helps me to focus, to remember what they have to go home to." She also calls every parent the first week of school just to talk and to thank them for doing a good job of raising their children. As Annette explains, "With a beginning like that, we can go on together because we're already supporting each other; we already have a past." June also contacts the children's parents every year through a letter in which she expresses her valuing of their family's culture and asks them to share with the class what is significant to their family. This dialogue continues through individual conversations with parents. Her example about becoming the teacher that many Jehovah Witnesses request reflects the trust that she generates.

Several of the teachers' narratives offer glimpses of the complexities involved in putting the principle of collaboration with parents into practice. Beth writes about the challenge she faced early on in her career that required balancing parents' "very different expectations for their children and the work we would do with them...." To meet this challenge, she recalls that she needed to "honor each child and each family's truths about themselves, and somehow balance those differences respectfully." Eric discusses how his own avoidance of conflict added another piece to the mix of creating collaborative relationships with families: "If I want to focus on family life in my curriculum, I'm not going to get far without involving [parents], and sometimes that creates conflict. But you can't get around it if you want to be effective, if you want to have a real impact on children's lives."

The failure to work with parents in the implementation of an anti-bias curriculum can result in a culture clash that leads to the loss of families from the program. Think, for example, of Beth's story of parental reactions to the way in which issues around gender identity and homophobia surfaced in the preschool classroom at her center: "The boy's parents were at my door the next morning. They were very upset. They belonged to a fundamentalist Christian church, and they didn't want their son to think that same-sex partners were even possible....Those parents pulled their kid out of the center....The next thing I knew I had two staff members in my office resigning, and another family left the next week....It was quite the upheaval, and that was how we began the conversation around anti-bias work with kids."

Eric describes the changes he went through in order to develop a more effective approach to relationships with parents: "I've spent a lot of time trying to 'educate' parents, but now I've had to ask, 'How much time have I spent finding out what they want their child to learn?'...To do that, I have to start lots of two-way discussions, and I have to develop trust. I have to focus on parents' issues, not mine, and model what I mean by respect." Eric also tells us that carrying out this approach did not come easily. He had to be critical of his past efforts, which primarily involved parents in support roles but not in planning their children's education. He had to learn not to "panic and get rigid and start sounding like an early childhood textbook about developmentally appropriate curriculum," but instead to learn from discussions about conflicts. Finally, Eric found that knowing who he is in the larger societal context makes it possible to understand the challenges in building trusting relationships: He discusses the necessity of accepting that "I am a white man, and I represent a powerful, mostly white institution, and that I can be clueless about other people's cultures and points of view." He also explains: "Many parents give me the benefit of the doubt, but it doesn't surprise me anymore when someone starts out on the defensive, expecting me to do something racist or sexist. It doesn't help if I get all huffy about that....I've realized that the burden of getting a trusting relationship going is on me."

Even with sincere and thoughtful effort, developing a collaborative relationship with all families around anti-bias education is not always possible. Prime examples of this kind of a breach are LaVita's stories of the white parents who refused to speak to African American staff members, did not want LaVita to hug their child, and were appalled at her teaching the children about Dr. Martin Luther King Jr. As she points out, many of these parents professed not wanting their children to grow up biased, but they were unable or unwilling to modify their own behavior to reach that end. In some cases, as LaVita found, the gap is so extreme that it cannot be bridged.

Resistance may also come from parents of color or poor parents who do not trust that anti-bias education will be safe and beneficial for their children. As Eric points out, this distrust is often based on "lousy experiences with institutions and with people in power. After all, parenting doesn't get much support or respect, mostly lip service. And memories of school aren't always positive." Through openness, patience, and engaging in regular dialogue, however, what may begin in disagreement or resistance can lead to everyone learning, growing, and collaborating on anti-bias work.

It is also helpful to keep in mind that many parents support the values and goals of anti-bias work. Remember Beth's story about the parent who supported her stand against homophobic attitudes, or Linda's story about the parent who stopped thinking of her daughters' lighter hair and skin as superior to her own darker hair and skin, or those parents at LaVita's school who began their own healing journey as a result of LaVita's anti-bias work.

Implications for Teachers

In all cases, building true partnerships with parents involves making the effort to understand their motivations for resisting or embracing anti-bias work, learning from them what they want for their children, and being willing to give up some of the power inherent in the teacher's role. In your relationships with parents and other family members, remember that perfection doesn't build trust, open communication and the willingness to hang in there does. And, through ongoing dialogue with parents, you will learn as much about yourself as you will about the children and families you serve.

Implications for Directors

You set the tone for building collaborative relationships between teachers and families. Create time in staff meetings for teachers to get clearer about their own cultural beliefs about children's development and how these affect their expectations and teaching styles. The points raised in the section about staff relationships are also relevant here. The foundation for power sharing with parents is a staff that feels safe to be vulnerable with each other, to make mistakes, to uncover their own biases, and to handle conflict. Begin the building of trust and partnership with families from the beginning of your program's year. Picking up the pieces after crisis arises is more difficult, although a crisis incident can be turned to positive use as a motivator for initiating the ongoing process of building new relationships among staff and families.

Implications for Teacher Educators

Although working effectively with parents is a cornerstone of early childhood philosophy, it is often one of the weaker areas of teacher education. From an anti-bias education perspective, a considerable portion of training must address the multiple skills and self-knowledge necessary to building open and collaborative relationships with families. Like staff and directors, teacher educators must shift their approach to families from a parent education model to a parent partnership model. This model will work most effectively if it is designed with some important considerations in mind. Among those are issues of cultural context, home language usage, the identification of family values, and a perspective that sees the teacher as learner as well as an educator and a resource.

10 Successful anti-bias education requires strategies for coping with the scope, seriousness, and challenges of the work.

All of the authors in this book discuss the all-encompassing nature of anti-bias work. As Barbara explains, "It's so easy to get overwhelmed because there's so much to do. Sometimes it feels almost as if the work is this huge octopus and you don't know where to grab on." All the contributors describe several strategies that have enabled them to stay in the work over the long haul:

Maintain a sense of perspective. It is important to listen and respond to other people, but it is also important not to lose who we are in others' views of us. When anti-bias educators are criticized or shunned for their beliefs, maintaining their sense of self and their perspective on the situation are of paramount importance. Barbara knew that she was perceived by other staff as the "multicultural watchdog." Rather than succumb to anger or hurt, she distanced herself from the immediate situation and mused, "That may not be all bad. Getting challenged more about anti-bias issues may mean we have more clout, or at least we are being perceived that way."

Use humor. Humor is one way to maintain one's perspective and equilibrium. Several of the teachers' stories describe their efforts with a humorous twist. Consider Barbara's comment on how she became aware of being an agent of change: "Through reflection and the experience of repeatedly beating my head against a brick wall, only to find that sometimes a tiny dent appears—in the wall." June advises us to "get a suit of armor!" for dealing with the slings and arrows of criticism. In a number of situations, humor lightened the load of pain and helped teachers to take disappointments less seriously and criticism less personally.

Pace yourself. Teachers learn that anti-bias work is not a headlong rush to some predetermined goal. As Barbara points out, "this is a marathon, not a sprint." In order to be an effective anti-bias educator, consider the particular goals you have and outcomes you want to achieve in your classroom and with your parents, staff, or group of children. The activities or approaches you select as vehicles for demonstrating anti-bias philosophy will be most effective if they take place in a sequence that uses previous experiences and information as a basis for new learning. Capturing moments of emergent curriculum that happen in the classroom, home, or community is an important part of seeing the work as whole, continuous, and abundant. It is neither necessary nor desirable to push ideas into one's program or curriculum. If teachers breath deeply, move steadily forward, and keep their eyes on the prize, all the while holding the hand of their allies, the work will get done. As Linda puts it: "There are times when doing this work is overwhelming, so I remember to choose my battles—knowing that I can't save the whole world, but I can contribute."

Celebrate small victories. Anti-bias work consists mostly of small steps toward change and only rarely of splashy events and visible transformations. Teachers and administrators learn to treasure small victories, as Beth did when a mother chose to register her baby at her center because of its anti-bias philosophy. Linda enjoyed telling how one mother changed to embrace an anti-bias philosophy in her parenting. And June was elated when a child told her, "I finally understand. Culture is all those things that we do with our family. All the things that we are. And race is just the way people look at us because of the color of our skin."

Consider the value of spiritual practice. For many people, a growing understanding of the world and the enormity of the social ills of our time sparks a journey of personal exploration and inner cleansing. These explorations often result in a spiritual search that can express itself in a variety of ways. It might lead to researching our ancestral beginnings, returning to rituals taught to us in childhood, or perhaps participating in traditional religious observances. Whatever form this search takes, the motivation seems similar—to find strength in the wisdom and traditions of past generations to stay the course. For example, Annette speaks of rediscovering her cultural spirituality and practicing meditation as a way of staying centered. She explains, "[I] have grown spiritually, and I believe this has opened up my mental capacity to learn new things and to be open to new people." LaVita describes how spirituality played an important role in her developmental process: "I enjoyed the work and was beginning to explore my faith. I felt spiritually full and had a purpose that made me soar in areas I had no idea I could reach." LaVita's faith also helped support her during hard times and connected her to the Ecumenical Child Care Network, with whom she is now happily working.

Implications for Teachers
Anti-bias work is difficult and can be discouraging. Humor can help teachers maintain their perspective and soften the blows of criticism and disappointment. Humor can also lighten a tense conversation and create openings for new thinking and connections. Of course, humor must be used carefully so that it does not contain oppressive overtones or create unintended victims. Teachers also must learn to pace themselves, to celebrate small victories, and to keep in mind the enormity and complexity of this work. One crucial strategy is to have a support group where members can help one another retain and sharpen their perspectives, equilibrium, and confidence.

Implications for Directors
Ways that directors can help teachers cope with the challenges of anti-bias work include gaining an awareness of and then acknowledging the stress levels that teachers are feeling, as well as providing outlets to dispel that stress, such as staff social events, personal days off, and help with stress management. Facilitating teachers' participation in networking events and professional development opportunities, such as anti-racism trainers' conferences, is valuable for both teachers and programs.

Implications for Teacher Educators

Including some class sessions on stress management and openly discussing the sources of teacher stress and burnout, while also providing information about resources for preventing them, can be a real support. Sharing struggles with similar issues and situations helps students understand the universality of their experience and brings teacher and students together as allies in the struggle for just, equitable education for all children.

11 Anti-bias teachers must have a support network.

All seven authors forcefully speak to the essential role support has played in their ability to begin and sustain their anti-bias work. Each teacher created and used one or more forms of support to express feelings, reflect, problem solve, get new ideas, and know that they are not alone in their work. The forms of support groups varied. Annette has a soul mate as well as her Circle of Girlfriends, all of whom work in her school. Linda, Annette, and June belong to support groups outside of their work sites. A telling moment for Linda was a confrontation with the rude waiter who insisted on calling her "mamacita." When she told her support group about the incident, they responded: "All right, Linda. You've got a voice. You've got a voice!" Linda describes the revelatory moment: "It was so exciting....Before that night I didn't really know that I had been developing my voice...."

Barbara has her work partner. In addition, she belongs to a CRAB group, originally organized as part of national project initiated by Louise Derman-Sparks and now carried on by its members. Eric's primary support group is the staff at his center. Family is another strong source of support for several of the authors.

Implications for Teachers

The main lesson to be drawn from these teachers' accounts is that support is essential, not just desirable. There are many ways teachers can create a support system for themselves. If they are fortunate enough to work at a supportive center, then their colleagues and the parents may fill that role. If they are at a center that lacks internal support, then they can look outside of the program. For example, they might organize a group of teachers from other programs in the same community.

Sometimes participation in a course or series of workshops will evolve into an ongoing support group. People may find it easier to talk with others with whom they share similar backgrounds or concerns and form a group around focusing on those issues (for example, single fathers, women of color, gay teachers). Teachers may find support from members of their local affiliate of the National Association of the Education of Young Children. Other national organizations that either have local chapters or informal networks include the National Coalition of Educational Activists, the Black Child Development Institute, the National Association of Bilingual Education, and the National Association of Multicultural Education. A national network of anti-bias educators and advocates is currently being organized (contact Louise Derman-Sparks at Pacific Oaks for further information). Religious and community organizations often have local support groups. For more informal support systems, teachers can turn to old friends, new friends, neighbors, and of course, family members. We have found the following characteristics to be common among successful anti-bias support groups: members have similar roles or work settings, regular meeting times are established, there is agreement on the format of meetings, there is a division of shared time (each participant has approximately the same amount of time to speak), and rules of respectful listening are established.

Implications for Directors

Directors are in the best position to encourage teachers to develop support systems. They might try to build a support group among the staff. If that seems impossible, then they can find out about local groups and encourage their teachers to explore those options. Directors need to honor their teachers' support systems. Evening meetings and weekend obligations should be planned in ways that minimize disruption of teachers' family time and their other support systems.

Implications for Teacher Educators

Teacher educators can encourage teachers and prospective teachers to participate in groups by providing names, phone numbers, and the Web page addresses of groups and individuals interested in meeting. They can invite teachers who participate in these groups to speak to their classes. In in-service or graduate courses, they can make a conscious effort to build a supportive group with the hope that the class might continue to meet even after the course is over.

12 Anti-bias work is joyful, healing, and empowering.

All the contributors to this book mention how much they had gained from doing anti-bias work. They spoke of many delights and a sense of accomplishment. As Beth summarizes, "For me, anti-bias work is about wholeness. It allows me to be the same person at work every day that I am at home; to keep intact the fabric of my convictions about children, equity, and social justice." Linda recalls, "There have been so many joyful moments—meeting so many good people, being able to stand up in front of people and talk, not letting my accent or mispronunciation of words silence me."

Anti-bias work has also been a healing process for people who had felt isolated and fragmented. June talks about becoming more comfortable with herself. Annette and Linda found that anti-bias work helped them to reclaim their cultures. Annette makes the following realization about how anti-bias work has shaped her life: "I used to keep things in categories. My teaching was separate from my home life. My home life was separate from my growth in meditation. And my support group was separate from everything else.... Through anti-bias work, my life has become whole."

Anti-bias work also empowers teachers. Barbara pushed herself to overcome her reluctance to speak in public. Linda's self-consciousness about her accent began to dissolve when she watched Mohammed gently confront the children who were laughing at his accent. Linda went on to teach and to become an outspoken advocate against all forms of oppression.

Implications for Teachers
Teachers need to track their growth, honor their accomplishments, and celebrate small victories. At the end of a day, a week, or a year, it is easy to recall only the failures and disappointments. Teachers should focus on enjoying and remembering the exhilarating moments as well as the long-term transformations that take place.

Implications for Directors
Directors might encourage staff to focus on their progress by creating a space in staff meetings for teachers to talk about something they feel really good about, perhaps an activity that went especially well or a good new connection with a parent. Asking questions (such as, "Why do you think it went so well?") offers a time for reflection that honors the work teachers are doing.

Directors can also support and validate teachers' growth by seeing them as resource people. They might encourage teachers to share an idea with the rest of the staff or to give a presentation either to the staff or to groups outside of the center. Teachers might initially be reluctant to take on these extra tasks and feel anxious about doing anything so public. As the stories in this book show, however, getting out into the world and making a public statement is a wonderfully empowering event.

Implications for Teacher Educators

In courses and workshops, teacher educators can provide feedback that helps students to focus on what they are learning and how much they have grown, rather than evaluating people in comparison to each other. They also can honor anti-bias classroom teachers by inviting them to share their experiences and expertise with students.

Conclusion

Anti-bias work is an engrossing process. It is more than a curriculum, more than a book, more than a course or a series of workshops. It is a way of life in which teachers synthesize their unique visions and worldviews with their love and caring for individual children and families. It requires each teacher to do the work in his or her own way.

It is a path with no end point. No one can ever say, "I have become an anti-bias teacher...or director...or teacher educator." Like peeling an endless onion, the layers of prejudice, privilege, and bias slowly dissolve as we work with children, talk with colleagues, learn from parents, and reflect on our lives.

It is a path with many turns, twists, ruts, and potholes. As all the teachers in this book describe, anti-bias work often evokes pain, confusion, and conflict. The disappointments and rejections are many, and almost everyone thinks about giving up at some point. Yet it is a path with much beauty along the way. All the contributors write of their joy in their own growing understanding and that of the children and families. They also savored their moments of success and their new sense of power when they overcame challenges.

Finally, anti-bias work is a path where we walk in companionship. All the teachers in this book mention the close bonds that they had formed with colleagues, children, and families as they struggled in their work. And through these relationships, they came to realize that no one does this work alone, that they travel with friends and, as Eric says, "a suitcase full of hope."

Other Anti-Bias Resources from Redleaf Press

Future Vision, Present Work: Learning from the Culturally Relevant Anti-Bias Leadership Project
Sharon Cronin, Louise Derman-Sparks, Sharon Henry, Cirecie Olatunji & Stacey York
Features stories from facilitators of cross-cultural advocacy work in Seattle, Minneapolis, and New Orleans.

Celebrate! An Anti-Bias Guide to Enjoying Holidays in Early Childhood Programs
By Julie Bisson
A bias-free guide filled with strategies for implementing exciting and developmentally appropriate holidays in your program.

Anti-Bias Books for Kids
Teaching Children New Ways to Know the People Around Them

> **Play Lady**
> **La Señora Juguetona**
> By Eric Hoffman
> Illustrated by Suzanne Tornquist
> The neighborhood children help Play Lady when she's the victim of a hate crime.

> **No Fair to Tigers**
> **No Es Justo Para los Tigres**
> By Eric Hoffman
> Illustrated by Janice Lee Porter
> Mandy and her stuffed tiger learn to ask for fair treatment.

> **Heroines and Heroes**
> **Heroínas y Héroes**
> By Eric Hoffman
> Illustrated by Judi Rosen
> Adventurous Kayla rescues Nate from the dragon in her backyard.

> **Best Best Colors**
> **Los Mejores Colores**
> By Eric Hoffman
> Illustrated by Celeste Henriquez
> Nate learns he can have more than one favorite color and one best friend.

To order or for a free catalog call: **1-800-423-8305**